ILLUSTRATED COURSE GUIDES

Verbal Communication

SECOND EDITION

COURSE TECHNOLOGY
CENGAGE Learning

Australia • Brazil • Japan • Korea • Mexico • Singapore • Spain • United Kingdom • United States

Jeff Butterfield

**Verbal Communication, 2nd Edition: Illustrated
Course Guide**
Jeff Butterfield

Executive Editor: Marjorie Hunt

Associate Acquisitions Editor: Amanda Lyons

Senior Product Manager: Christina Kling Garrett

Associate Product Manager: Kim Klasner

Editorial Assistant: Brandelynn Perry

Director of Marketing: Elisa Roberts

Marketing Manager: Julie Schuster

Marketing Coordinator: Adrienne Fung

Contributing Author: Lisa Ruffolo

Developmental Editor: Lisa Ruffolo

Content Project Manager: GEX Publishing Services

Proofreader: Brandy Lilly

Indexer: Elizabeth Cunningham

Print Buyer: Fola Orekoya

Composition: GEX Publishing Services

For product information and technology assistance, contact us at
Cengage Learning Customer & Sales Support, 1-800-354-9706
For permission to use material from this text or product, submit all requests online at **cengage.com/permissions**
Further permissions questions can be emailed to
permissionrequest@cengage.com

Library of Congress Control Number: 2012931047

ISBN-10: 1-133-52652-7
ISBN-13: 978-1-133-52652-0

Course Technology
20 Channel Center Street
Boston, Massachusetts 02210
USA

Cengage Learning is a leading provider of customized learning solutions with office locations around the globe, including Singapore, the United Kingdom, Australia, Mexico, Brazil, and Japan. Locate your local office at:
international.cengage.com/region

Cengage Learning products are represented in Canada by Nelson Education, Ltd.

To learn more about Course Technology, visit **www.cengage.com/coursetechnology**

To learn more about Cengage Learning, visit **www.cengage.com**

Purchase any of our products at your local college store or at our preferred online store
www.cengagebrain.com

Printed at EPAC, USA, 08-16

About the Series

Students work hard to earn certificates and degrees to prepare for a particular career—but do they have the soft skills necessary to succeed in today's digital workplace? Can they communicate effectively? Present themselves professionally? Work in a team? Industry leaders agree there is a growing need for these essential soft skills; in fact, they are critical to a student's success in the workplace. Without them, students will struggle and even fail. However, students entering the workforce who can demonstrate strong soft skills have a huge competitive advantage.

The *Illustrated Course Guides—Soft Skills for a Digital Workplace* series is designed to help you teach these important skills, better preparing your students to enter a competitive marketplace. Here are some of the key elements you will find in each book in the series:

- **Focused content allows for flexibility:** Each book in the series is short and focused, covering only the most essential skills related to the topic. You can use the modular content in standalone courses or workshops or you can integrate it into existing courses.

- **Visual design keeps students engaged:** Our unique pedagogical design presents each skill on two facing pages, with key concepts and instructions on the left and illustrations on the right. This keeps students of all levels on track.

- **Varied activities put skills to the test:** Each book includes hands-on activities, team exercises, critical thinking questions, and scenario-based activities to allow students to put their skills to work and demonstrate their retention of the material.

- **Online activities engage students:** A companion Web site provides engaging online activities that give students instant feedback and reinforce the skills in the book. Engagement Tracker lets instructors monitor student progress.

Read the Preface for more details on the key pedagogical elements and features of this book. We hope the books in this series help your students gain the critical soft skills they need to succeed in whatever career they choose.

Advisory Board

We thank our Advisory Board who gave us their opinions and guided our decisions for the second editions. They are as follows:

Paulette Gannett – SUNY – Broome Community College
Sherry Sparrowk – Peninsula College
Audrey Styer – Morton College
Charlene West – Durham Technical Community College

Preface

Welcome to *Verbal Communication, Second Edition: Illustrated Course Guides*. If this is your first experience with the Illustrated Course Guides, you'll see that this book has a unique design: each skill is presented on two facing pages, with Essential Elements on the left and illustrations and examples pictured on the right. The layout makes it easy to learn a skill without having to read a lot of text and flip pages to see an illustration. The design also makes this a great reference after the course is over! See the illustration on the right to learn more about the pedagogical and design elements of a typical chapter.

Focused on the Essentials

Each two-page lesson presents only the most important information about the featured skill. The left page of the lesson presents about five key Essential Elements, which are the most important guidelines that a student needs to know about the skill. Absorbing and retaining a limited number of key ideas makes it more likely that students will retain and apply the skill in a real-life situation.

Hands-On Activities

Every Essential Elements lesson contains a You Try It exercise, where students demonstrate their understanding of the lesson skill by completing a task that relates to it. The steps in the You Try It exercises are often general, requiring that students use critical thinking to complete the task.

Real World Advice and Examples

To help put lesson skills in context, many lessons contain yellow shaded boxes that present real-world stories pulled from today's workplace. Some lessons also contain Do's and Don'ts tables, featuring key guidelines on what to do and not do in certain workplace situations relating to the lesson skill. The Technology @ Work lesson at the end of every part covers Web 2.0 tools and other technologies relating to the part.

Each two-page spread focuses on a single learning objective.

Short introduction reviews key lesson points and presents a real-world case study to engage students.

Objective 3 Part 1

Understanding Nonverbal Language

Besides words and tone, nonverbal cues contribute to spoken communication. Body language and gestures add meaning to your message. Nonverbal language includes hand and arm motions, eye contact and movement, facial expressions, the position of your body, and your overall appearance. Your audience perceives nonverbal language as part of your message, and uses it to determine how to interpret your words. Being more aware of body language and nonverbal cues helps you be a more effective listener and speaker. Table 1-3 summarizes do's and don'ts for using nonverbal language. Figure 1-3 shows examples of nonverbal language in the workplace. **case** As you rehearse your presentation for the career fair, Juan Ramirez gives you a few pointers about your body language and nonverbal communication.

ESSENTIAL ELEMENTS

QUICK TIP
Prolonged eye contact, however, can make your listener uncomfortable.

1. **Maintain eye contact**
Eye movements send signals that help regulate the flow of information between people. Your eyes can show interest, understanding, happiness, confusion, anxiety, and fear. Make eye contact to establish credibility and show you are engaged with your audience. People trust you when you look directly at them as you speak, and are skeptical if you don't maintain eye contact.

2. **Present pleasant facial expressions**
The human smile is a powerful cue that signals friendliness, happiness, warmth, and acceptance. If you smile frequently when you are talking with others, they perceive you as approachable, appealing, and friendly. They are also likely to react positively to your message and remember what you say. A frown or grimace also sends a powerful message, though it is often negative.

QUICK TIP
Gestures vary from culture to culture. What is meaningful in one country may not be in another.

3. **Gesture appropriately**
People usually move their arms, hands, and fingers when they speak. Effective communicators use physical gestures to emphasize important points. Appropriate gestures can enliven and animate what you say and help to communicate your enthusiasm and sincerity. If you do not move at all when you speak, others might perceive you as boring or tense.

4. **Maintain good posture**
Your posture is your body's position when you are sitting, standing, or walking. Posture communicates your mood, attitude, and interest in a topic. When communicating with others, sit or stand with an erect (but not stiff) posture, which sends a message of confidence and competence. Lean slightly towards your listeners to show you are receptive and interested in what they have to say. Avoid speaking when your back is turned or you are distracted with another task because this signals disinterest and insincerity.

QUICK TIP
Signs of discomfort in your listeners include looking away, stepping backwards, turning their body at an angle to you, or folding their arms over their chest.

5. **Keep your distance**
In communication, **proximity** is how physically close you are to your audience. Maintaining appropriate proximity is an important part of verbal communication. People expect you to respect their personal space and feel uncomfortable if you intrude on it. Appropriate proximity is affected by the relationship you have with the listener, the type of communication (intimate, friendly, professional, or public speaking), and your cultural norms. If you notice signs of discomfort that suggest you've moved into your listener's space, immediately increase the distance between you and your listener.

YOU TRY IT

Plan to use nonverbal cues when you speak. Open the VC1-Y3.docx document and follow the steps in the worksheet. When you are finished, submit the document to your instructor as requested.

Verbal Communication 6   Understanding the Basics of Verbal Communication

You Try It activities let students perform tasks to demonstrate their understanding of the lesson objective.

Essential Elements present key points that students need to know to perform the lesson skill successfully.

Every lesson features large illustrations of examples discussed in the lesson.

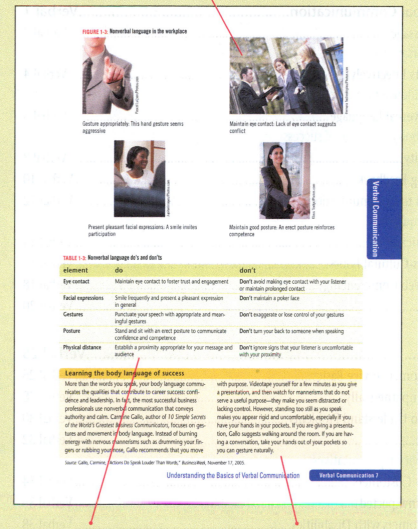

Lessons and Exercises

This book is divided into five parts, with each part containing about eight 2-page lessons, or learning objectives. The lessons use Quest Specialty Travel, a fictional adventure travel company, as the case study. The assignments on the peach pages at the end of each part increase in difficulty. Data files and case studies provide a variety of interesting and relevant business applications. Assignments include:

- **Soft Skills Reviews** provide multiple choice questions that test students' understanding of the part material.

- **Critical Thinking Questions** pose topics for discussion that require analysis and evaluation. Many also challenge students to consider and react to realistic critical thinking and application of the part skills.

- **Independent Challenges** are case projects requiring critical thinking and application of the part skills.

- **Real Life Independent Challenges** are practical exercises where students can apply the skills they learned in an activity that will help their own lives. For instance, they might create a resume, write a letter to a potential employer, or role play for a job interview for their dream position.

- **Team Challenges** are practical projects that require working together in a team to solve a problem.

- **Be the Critic Exercises** are activities that require students to evaluate a flawed example and provide ideas for improving it.

Do's & Don'ts tables present key tips for what to do and not do.

News to Use boxes provide real-world stories related to the lesson topic.

Contents

Preface iv

Verbal Communication

Part 1: Understanding the Basics of Verbal Communication..Verbal 1

    1: Organizing Your Messages... Verbal 2
       Crucial conversations

    2: Using Vocal Elements Effectively... Verbal 4
       Building confidence in public speaking

    3: Understanding Nonverbal Language.. Verbal 6
       Learning the body language of success

    4: Developing Credibility... Verbal 8

    5: Giving and Receiving Feedback .... Verbal 10

    6: Overcoming Barriers to Communication .... Verbal 12
       Voice mail etiquette

    7: Communicating Ethically... Verbal 14

    8: Understanding Cross-Cultural Issues.. Verbal 16

    Technology @ Work: Web Conferencing .... Verbal 18

    Practice .... Verbal 20

Part 2: Working with Customers ....Verbal 25

    9: Understanding Customer Service Basics.. Verbal 26

    10: Communicating Empathetically .... Verbal 28

    11: Asking Questions to Understand Problems .... Verbal 30

    12: Denying Requests.. Verbal 32
       Customer service representatives

    13: Coping with Angry Customers .... Verbal 34

    14: Dealing with the Unexpected .... Verbal 36

    15: Working with Customers with Disabilities..................................... Verbal 38
       Telephone etiquette when talking to customers with disabilities

    Technology @ Work: Internet Monitoring.. Verbal 40

    Practice .... Verbal 42

Part 3: Developing Professional Telephone Skills ....Verbal 47

    16: Exploring Professional Telephone Communication............................ Verbal 48

    17: Placing Telephone Calls .... Verbal 50

18: Receiving Telephone Calls .... Verbal 52
    Text message etiquette

19: Using Voice Mail .... Verbal 54

20: Leaving Professional Messages .... Verbal 56
    Instant interruptions

21: Taking Calls for Other People .... Verbal 58

22: Screening, Holding, and Transferring Calls .... Verbal 60

23: Developing Cell Phone Etiquette.. Verbal 62

Technology @ Work: Voice over Internet Protocol .... Verbal 64

Practice .... Verbal 66

Part 4: Improving Informal Communication .... Verbal 73

24: Communicating Informally.. Verbal 74
    You heard it on the grapevine

25: Listening Actively... Verbal 76

26: Speaking Persuasively... Verbal 78

27: Negotiating Effectively... Verbal 80

28: Managing Conflict .... Verbal 82

29: Participating in Meetings .... Verbal 84
    Take charge of your meetings

30: Dealing with Office Politics .... Verbal 86

31: Making Proper Introductions.. Verbal 88

Technology @ Work: Microblogging Tools .... Verbal 90

Practice .... Verbal 92

Part 5: Making Formal Presentations .... Verbal 97

32: Planning Effective Presentations .... Verbal 98
    Presentation design tips

33: Developing Presentation Content .... Verbal 100

34: Rehearsing a Presentation .... Verbal 102

35: Delivering a Presentation .... Verbal 104
    Delivering presentations to three types of audiences

36: Building Rapport .... Verbal 106

37: Managing Anxiety.. Verbal 108

38: Using Appropriate Visuals .... Verbal 110

39: Managing Questions and Answers... Verbal 112

Technology @ Work: Presentation Software .... Verbal 114

Practice .... Verbal 116

Glossary 1

Index 3

CourseMate

This text includes access to a robust premium Web site called CourseMate. Cengage Learning's CourseMate brings course concepts to life with interactive learning, study, and exam preparation tools that support the printed textbook. CourseMate includes an integrated eBook with audio, quizzes, review cards, scenario videos, and more! Use these activities to assess and enhance student learning.

- **Video Introductions** explain what the student will learn and why the lesson content is important.
- **eBook with video** provides author insights and allows the student to listen to the text.
- **Scenario Videos** show the key tasks in the lesson done well and done poorly, and then quizzes the student on what they learned.
- **Review Cards** allow students to review the key learning elements.
- **Capstone Exercises** allow students to review what they learned by completing a Soft Skills Review quiz, answering Critical Thinking Questions, and more!
- **Career Transitions** gives students the resources to search for a job in real time, create a resume, and prepare for an interview using interview simulations.

Information on how to access the CourseMate for this book is available in *Getting Started with CourseMate* on page ix.

Instructor Resources

The Instructor Resources CD is Course Technology's way of putting the resources and information needed to teach and learn effectively into your hands. With an integrated array of teaching and learning tools that offer you and your students a broad range of technology-based instructional options, we believe this CD represents the highest quality and most cutting edge resources available to instructors today. Many of these resources are available at www.cengage.com/coursetechnology. The resources available with this book are:

- **Instructor's Manual**—Available as an electronic file, the Instructor's Manual is a valuable teaching tool for your course. It includes detailed lecture topics with teaching tips for each part.

- **Sample Syllabus**—Prepare and customize your course easily using this sample course outline.

- **PowerPoint Presentations**—Each part has a corresponding PowerPoint presentation that you can use in lecture, distribute to your students, or customize to suit your course.

- **Figure Files**—The figures in the text are provided on the Instructor Resources CD to help you illustrate key topics or concepts. You can create traditional overhead transparencies by printing the figure files. Or you can create electronic slide shows by using the figures in a presentation program such as PowerPoint.

- **Solutions to Exercises**—Solutions to Exercises contains every file students are asked to create or modify in the lessons

and end-of-part material. This section also includes a solutions to the Soft Skills Reviews and Independent Challenges.

- **Data Files for Students**—To complete most of the exercises in this book, your students will need Data Files. You can post the Data Files on a file server for students to copy. The Data Files are available on the Instructor Resources CD-ROM, the Review Pack, and can also be downloaded from www.cengage.com/coursetechnology.

- **Test Banks**—ExamView is a powerful testing software package that allows you to create and administer printed, computer (LAN-based). ExamView test banks are pre-loaded with questions that correspond to the topics covered in this text, enabling students to generate detailed study guides that include page references for further review. Test banks are also available in Blackboard and WebCT formats.

Getting Started with CourseMate

This book is designed to work together with CourseMate, an online companion containing videos, interactive exercises, practice tests, flash cards, and other resources to help you learn the skills in this book and keep you engaged. CourseMate also contains a media-rich e-book version of the text that you can search, mark up with notes, and highlight. **case** The lessons in this section provide an overview of CourseMate and step by step instructions on how to access it. In order to access the CourseMate for this book, you need a pin code. (If you do not have a pin code, see your instructor.)

OBJECTIVES

1 Understanding CourseMate

2 Accessing CourseMate

3 Using CourseMate

Understanding CourseMate

Cengage Learning's CourseMate brings course concepts to life with interactive learning, study, and exam preparation tools that support the printed textbook. CourseMate includes an integrated eBook with audio and interactive teaching and learning tools. These tools include quizzes, review cards, scenario videos, and Career Transitions, which give students the resources to search for a job, create a resume, and prepare for an interview. To use CourseMate, you must first purchase a CourseMate access code for this book. You also need a Web browser and must be connected to the Internet. **case** This lesson reviews the key elements of the CourseMate for this book.

DETAILS

The CourseMate for this book includes the following elements:

- **Video Introductions**

  The CourseMate includes short video introductions for each two-page lesson in the text. Each video runs about 1 minute long and provides a context to help you understand why the skill is important. See Figure 1.

- **eBook with Audio**

  The eBook lets you read each two-page lesson of the text on your computer screen. You can search for specific topics or keywords, highlight text, and take notes. You can also listen to an audio version of text, which includes extra insights from the author.

- **Scenario Videos**

  For each two-page lesson, you can watch two scenario videos that run about two minutes each. The Good Job video shows the tasks from the lesson done well, and the Bad Job video shows the tasks from the lesson done poorly. You also have the option to quiz yourself on the soft skill flaws in the Bad Job video. See Figure 2.

- **You Try It Exercises**

  You Try It exercises are in worksheet format so you can easily complete a task that relates to the skills in the two-page lesson. See Figure 3.

- **Practice Tests**

  Practice Tests allow you to test yourself on what you just learned.

- **Review Cards**

  Use the Review Cards to master the key learning elements in each part. The Review Cards present questions on one side of a digital card and answers on the other.

- **Technology @ Work**

  Use the Technology @ Work hands-on exercises to learn about Web 2.0 tools and other technologies.

- **Capstone Exercises**

  Capstone Exercises test you on multiple learning objectives. Review what you learned in each part by completing the Soft Skills Review multiple-choice quiz. Critical Thinking Questions introduce topics for discussion and are available in worksheet format so you can discuss them easily. Independent Challenges, Real Life Independent Challenges, Team Challenges, and Be the Critic exercises allow you to practice your skills and are available as downloadable PDF files.

- **Data Files**

  Data Files for each activity in the book are available in a zip file for download.

- **Career Transitions**

  The CourseMate gives you access to Career Transitions, a site that gives you the resources to search for a job, create a quality resume, write an effective cover letter, and prepare for an interview with interview simulations.

FIGURE 1

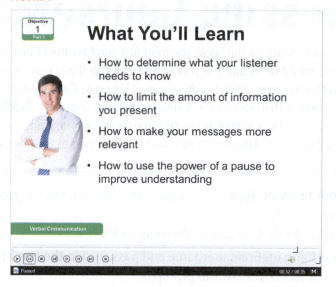

FIGURE 2

FIGURE 3

Objective 2
CourseMate

Accessing CourseMate

To access the CourseMate for this book, you must first purchase the CourseMate access code for this book. The access code might be included in your course materials if you purchased them at your school's bookstore. Then, with your access code handy, you must log on to CengageBrain, a Web site for accessing various student resources that accompany Cengage Learning textbooks. **case** In this lesson, you set up a CengageBrain user profile and establish a username and password, if necessary. Then you enter your access code to access the CourseMate. (Note: You must be connected to the Internet to perform these steps.)

STEPS

1. **Open your browser, type http://login.cengagebrain.com in your browser's Address bar, then press [Enter]**
   The Login page for the CengageBrain site opens. See Figure 4.

TROUBLE
If you don't have a CengageBrain username and password, click Create an Account, then follow the prompts to create one.

2. **Type your CengageBrain username and password in the Log in section of the page**
   The Find your Textbook or Materials page opens.

3. **Type your access code in the box below Have Another Product to Register?, then click Register**
   The CengageBrain site accepts your access code and the cover and title of the book you're using appears under My Courses & Materials.

4. **Click Open next to CourseMate for the title of the book you're using.**
   The CourseMate page opens. See Figure 5.

FIGURE 4

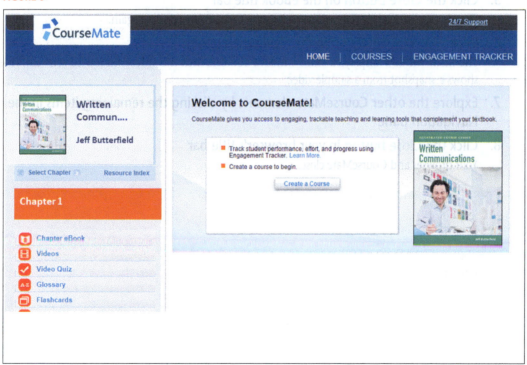

FIGURE 5

Objective
3
CourseMate

Using CourseMate

CourseMate is a great study tool that helps you learn and master the content you need to succeed in this course. In addition to interactive learning and study aids, CourseMate comes with Engagement Tracker, a tool that lets your instructor monitor student engagement in the course. Your instructor might provide you with a Course Key, which you need to enter to use Engagement Tracker. (If your instructor chooses not to use Engagement Tracker, you can still access all the content on CourseMate.) **case** In this lesson, you learn the basics of using CourseMate.

STEPS

1. **If your instructor provided you with a Course Key, click Enter Your Course Key (or skip to Step 3 if your instructor did not provide you with a Course Key)**

   The Enter Your Course Key dialog box opens, as shown in Figure 6.

2. **Type your Course Key, then click Submit**

3. **Click Select a Chapter, just below the book cover on the left side of the screen**

   The full table of contents for the book appears in the Select a Chapter window. You can open this window anytime you want to access the content for a particular chapter.

4. **Click outside the Select a Chapter window, click eBook with Audio, then click Access the eBook**

   After a moment, a new window opens and displays an eBook version of this text. You can navigate through the eBook content using the Table of Contents, glossary, or index. You can search for words or phrases and annotate the text.

5. **Click the Close button on the eBook title bar**

   The eBook closes, and your screen displays the CourseMate window again.

6. **Click Video Introduction in the Navigation pane**

   The main window displays a video window. You can click the video window to start the video. Figure 7 shows a snapshot from a sample video.

7. **Explore the other CourseMate elements by clicking the remaining items in the Navigation pane**

8. **Click the Close button in your browser's title bar**

   Your browser and CourseMate close.

FIGURE 6

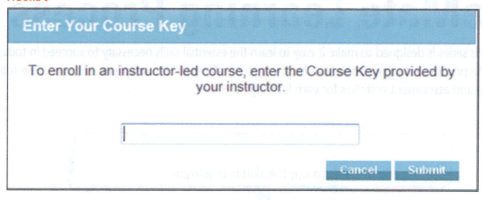

FIGURE 7

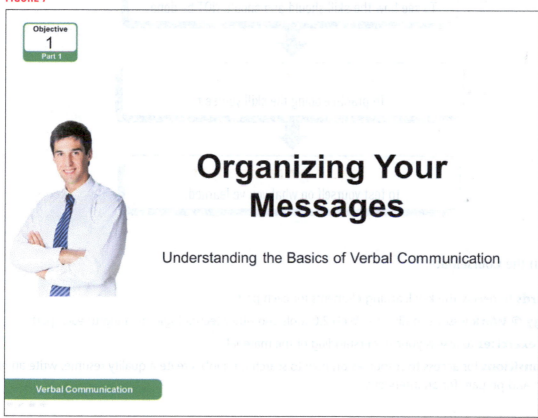

CourseMate Learning Process

The Illustrated Soft Skills series is designed to make it easy to learn the essential skills necessary to succeed in today's competitive workplace. CourseMate provides engaging tools that help you learn efficiently and keep you engaged. The following graphic shows the five learning and assessment activities for each learning objective.

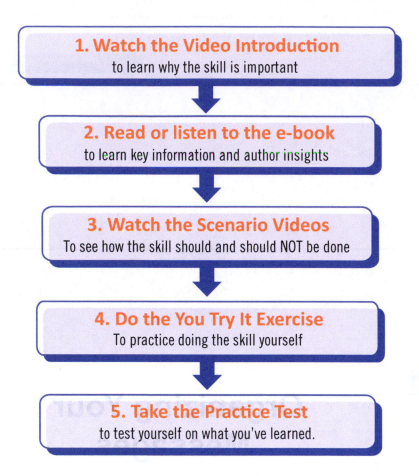

1. Watch the Video Introduction
to learn why the skill is important

2. Read or listen to the e-book
to learn key information and author insights

3. Watch the Scenario Videos
To see how the skill should and should NOT be done

4. Do the You Try It Exercise
To practice doing the skill yourself

5. Take the Practice Test
to test yourself on what you've learned.

Also available in the CourseMate:

- **Review cards** to review the key learning elements for each part.
- **Technology @ Work** lessons to discover Web 2.0 tools and other technologies relating to each part.
- **Capstone exercises** to assess your understanding of the material.
- **Career Transitions** for access to resources on how to search for a job, create a quality resume, write an effective cover letter, and prepare for an interview.

Part 1

Understanding the Basics of Verbal Communication

Files You Will Need:

VC1-Y2.docx

VC1-Y3.docx

VC1-Y4.docx

VC1-Y5.docx

VC1-Y6.docx

VC1-Y7.docx

VC1-Y8.docx

VC1-TechWork.docx

VC1-IC1.docx

VC1-IC2.docx

Verbal communication involves using speech to exchange information with others. You usually communicate verbally in face-to-face conversations. Meetings, interviews, conferences, speeches, and phone calls are other forms of verbal communication. In business, you communicate verbally to exchange ideas, understand diverse points of view, and solve problems. Because verbal skills are among those most valued by employers, developing these skills will help you find jobs, advance your career, and improve your professional performance. **case** You are an administrative assistant in the Human Resources Department of Quest Specialty Travel. Juan Ramirez, the director of Human Resources, is attending a career fair at a local community college. He wants you to attend as his assistant, give a short talk on working in the travel industry, and be available at the Quest table to answer questions. He suggests that you focus on your speaking skills in the weeks before the career fair.

OBJECTIVES

1 Organize your messages

2 Use vocal elements effectively

3 Understand nonverbal language

4 Develop credibility

5 Give and receive feedback

6 Overcome barriers to communication

7 Communicate ethically

8 Understand cross-cultural issues

Yuri Arcurs/Shutterstock.com

Organizing Your Messages

In **verbal communication**, or oral communication, one person sends a message to another person or group using speech. Communication is successful only when the speaker and listener understand each other. Because the average person is exposed to thousands of messages every day, your message must stand out to catch your listener's attention. After receiving the message, your listener must be able to interpret, or **decode**, its meaning. Effective communicators organize their messages so they are clear, logical, and easy for the listener to understand. Figure 1-1 outlines the communication process. As shown in Table 1-1, some messages are appropriate for spoken communication, while others are more suited for written communication. **case** You are preparing to attend the career fair at a local community college to talk about the travel industry. You meet with Juan Ramirez to discuss how you should organize your talk.

DETAILS

Keep the following details in mind to organize your messages and clarify their meaning:

QUICK TIP
If your main idea is especially important, also conclude your message with it.

- ### Start with what your listener needs to know

  Your listener is most likely to remember the first and last parts of your message. Before you speak with someone, identify the purpose of your discussion—the purpose becomes your main idea. Start the conversation with what your listener needs to know, then move to the supporting information.

- ### Limit the amount of information

  People have a limited capacity to listen to and decipher a message, especially if they are distracted by noisy surroundings, interruptions, or other communication obstacles. Packing too much information into a conversation can leave your listeners confused or remembering only part of what you said. Limit the amount of information you convey in a single interaction. In a one-on-one conversation, for example, express one main idea and up to three supporting ideas. If you need to share more information, do so in separate discussions.

QUICK TIP
In verbal communication, the average adult can best understand language composed at a sixth-grade reading level.

- ### Eliminate unnecessary words

  It can take more concentration to understand spoken words than written ones. When you use complicated language or unnecessary words, you make it difficult for your listener to interpret what you are saying. Use simple sentences, and avoid technical language and jargon whenever possible.

- ### Make your messages relevant to your listener

  Although it is natural to discuss subjects you consider important, if your listener has different priorities, your message might not be well received. Frame your ideas so they are relevant to your listeners. Adopt their point of view, then explain or show how your subject is beneficial to them.

- ### Take a direct approach

  Your listeners have to manage several tasks as they listen to you. They must pay attention to what you are saying, interpret your nonverbal signals, ignore noise and other distractions, and make sense of incoming information. To help your listeners, take a direct approach by introducing your subject, explaining what you want, and identifying your expectations. Be polite and tactful, but don't make your audience guess what you mean.

QUICK TIP
Look and listen for feedback from your listeners to make sure they understand your message.

- ### Plan for short breaks

  As you communicate, plan to stop occasionally so your audience can absorb your message, especially after you make an important point, request action, or introduce a new subject. Use these short breaks to review the body language of your listeners and gauge their understanding. However, avoid long pauses, which can make your listeners feel uncomfortable.

FIGURE 1-1: Spoken communication process

Speaker → Message → Encode → Message → Channel → Message → Decode → Message → Listener

Encode: Convert to words and gestures

Channel: Speak face-to-face or on the phone

Decode: Interpret words and gestures

Feedback

TABLE 1-1: Appropriate uses for spoken communication

you want to:	use spoken	use written
Receive an immediate answer	•	
Congratulate a colleague	•	
Be sure your audience interprets your message correctly	•	
Negotiate with others to build a consensus	•	
Minimize misunderstandings when providing information	•	
Allow your audience to ask questions to clarify information	•	
Promote a close or friendly working relationship	•	
Maintain a record of the communication		•
Save time when providing a response		•
Avoid interrupting your colleague		•
Deliver a formal message		•

Crucial conversations

On her FlatWorld Knowledge Web site (*www.flatworldknowledge.com*), Talya Bauer identifies conversations such as asking for a raise or promoting a project as crucial conversations, where the stakes and emotions are high. She lists 10 recommendations for improving the quality of your conversations, especially crucial ones:

1. *Be the first to say hello*: Introduce yourself to others, clearly pronouncing your name so everyone catches it.
2. *Use names*: Listen for the names of your conversation partners and use them when addressing others.
3. *Think before you speak*: Instead of speaking quickly to fill pauses, take time to think instead of blundering into a mistake.
4. *Be receptive to new ideas*: If you disagree with an idea, learn more about it. Say, "That's interesting," instead of "I don't agree."
5. *Listen*: Listen as much as you speak, if not more.
6. *Ask questions*: Draw others out as necessary by asking thoughtful questions.
7. *Make eye contact*: Show others that you are engaged and focused on what they are saying.
8. *Repeat or paraphrase*: In your own words, repeat what others say to make sure you understand.
9. *Keep it brief*: Instead of monopolizing someone's time, leave them feeling that another conversation with you would be interesting and productive.
10. *Be prepared*: Before a crucial conversation, anticipate what others might say or ask. Prepare questions and facts ahead of time.

Source: Bauer, T., Organizational Behavior. Retrieved October 28, 2011 from *www.flatworldknowledge.com*.

Using Vocal Elements Effectively

In a conversation, your voice is the medium, or **channel**, you use to communicate with others. People not only listen to the words you say, but the way you say them—these are the **vocal elements** of your speech. Vocal elements include voice inflections, rate of speech, volume, and tone. They can add interest and meaning to your messages. Using vocal elements that are appropriate for your purpose and audience can make your words more appealing and powerful, causing others to pay attention to what you say. Table 1-2 summarizes the do's and don'ts of using vocal elements. ◄case► You have a good idea of what you want to say during your short presentation at the career fair. Juan Ramirez suggests you also rehearse how to use vocal elements effectively.

ESSENTIAL ELEMENTS

1. Change the speed of your voice

People who consistently speak at the same pace tend to be dull and ineffective communicators. Those who vary the rate of their spoken words are more interesting. In addition, the rate of your speech signals how listeners should interpret your words. Speak quickly and use an enthusiastic tone to excite your listeners. Speak slowly when you want your audience to absorb your words or anticipate the next idea.

> **QUICK TIP**
> In professional settings, pitch your voice slightly lower than your casual speaking voice.

2. Shift the pitch of your voice

Voice **pitch** is the frequency of speech. Both high and low pitches are useful at times, though you should not take either to an extreme. Raising the pitch of your voice signals uncertainty or suggests a question. Lowering the pitch gives your voice a more authoritative and influential character.

3. Control the volume of your voice

The volume of your voice affects how well your listeners can hear and understand you. Speak loud enough so that your audience can hear you comfortably. If the volume is much louder, your voice might annoy your listener and disturb others. Speaking too softly makes your words hard to hear and communicates timidity and submissiveness. Varying your volume adds character to your speech, so raise the volume when you want to emphasize a word or phrase. Lower your voice to dramatize an idea or let your listener concentrate on what you are saying.

> **QUICK TIP**
> Catch your breath when you pause to make the silence seem natural.

4. Punctuate with pauses

Effective speakers pause occasionally to break up the flow of information so that listeners can process and understand what was said. A good time to pause briefly is after you make an important point or conclude an idea. You can also use pauses to create anticipation. Figure 1-2 shows that the most effective combination of vocal elements is low pitch with a varied pace and occasional pauses.

> **QUICK TIP**
> If enunciating is difficult for you, try speaking more slowly than normal.

5. Articulate your words

To improve your listeners' understanding, clearly enunciate each sentence, phrase, and word. You can improve your pronunciation through conscious practice. When you speak clearly, you convey competence, confidence, and intelligence.

YOU TRY IT

Practice using vocal elements effectively by rehearsing one side of a conversation. Open the **VC1-Y2.docx** document and follow the steps in the worksheet. When you are finished, submit the document to your instructor as requested.

FIGURE 1-2: Effective vocal elements

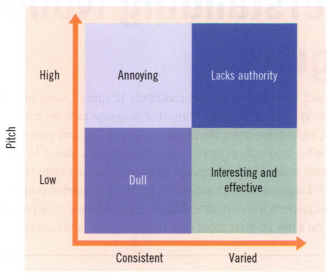

TABLE 1-2: Vocal elements do's and don'ts

element	do	don't
Speed	• Speak quickly to excite your listeners • Speak slowly to help your audience absorb your words and ideas	**Don't** speak only at one pace
Pitch	• Raise the pitch of your voice to ask a question • Lower the pitch of your voice to convey authority and influence	**Don't** use a very high or very low pitch
Volume	• Raise the volume of your voice to emphasize a word or phrase • Lower the volume of your voice to dramatize an idea or help listeners concentrate on your words	• **Don't** speak so loudly that the volume is uncomfortable for your audience • **Don't** speak so softly that your words are difficult to hear
Flow	• Pause occasionally to let listeners catch up with what you said	**Don't** pause so long that the silence seems unnatural
Articulation	• Clearly enunciate each sentence, phrase, and word	**Don't** overlook how you pronounce words

Building confidence in public speaking

One form of oral communication is public speaking, which is perennially named as a top fear in the American workplace. You can overcome some of this fear and project confidence by tuning your voice. In addition to the three Ps of vocal tuning—pace, pitch, and pauses—Douglas Anderson, president of Your Voice Coach, adds one more: passion. "This all-important quality will be the biggest selling point you have," he says. "Love your topic." Anderson recommends eliminating nasality by yawning to open and relax your throat and palate. Your posture also affects your speaking voice. "Stand straight, relax, and let your breath come in down low," Anderson suggests. "It should feel like it's entering your body around your waist, not being pulled down your throat." Continue to be aware of your breath to relax yourself. If your voice sounds too high, clipped, or nervous, breathe low and loosen your shoulders. Keep your throat open. "An open throat protects your voice and produces a richer sound," Anderson says. The sound of your calm, confident voice will put you and your audience at ease.

Source: Anderson, Douglas, "10 Tips for a Power Voice: Make your voice one of your best assets," *Entrepreneur*, August 30, 2007.

Understanding Nonverbal Language

Besides words and tone, nonverbal cues contribute to spoken communication. Body language and gestures add meaning to your message. Nonverbal language includes hand and arm motions, eye contact and movement, facial expressions, the position of your body, and your overall appearance. Your audience perceives nonverbal language as part of your message, and uses it to determine how to interpret your words. Being more aware of body language and nonverbal cues helps you be a more effective listener and speaker. Table 1-3 summarizes do's and don'ts for using nonverbal language. Figure 1-3 shows examples of nonverbal language in the workplace. **case** As you rehearse your presentation for the career fair, Juan Ramirez gives you a few pointers about your body language and nonverbal communication.

ESSENTIAL ELEMENTS

QUICK TIP
Prolonged eye contact, however, can make your listener uncomfortable.

1. Maintain eye contact

Eye movements send signals that help regulate the flow of information between people. Your eyes can show interest, understanding, happiness, confusion, anxiety, and fear. Make eye contact to establish credibility and show you are engaged with your audience. People trust you when you look directly at them as you speak, and are skeptical if you don't maintain eye contact.

2. Present pleasant facial expressions

The human smile is a powerful cue that signals friendliness, happiness, warmth, and acceptance. If you smile frequently when you are talking with others, they perceive you as approachable, appealing, and friendly. They are also likely to react positively to your message and remember what you say. A frown or grimace also sends a powerful message, though it is often negative.

QUICK TIP
Gestures vary from culture to culture. What is meaningful in one country may not be in another.

3. Gesture appropriately

People usually move their arms, hands, and fingers when they speak. Effective communicators use physical gestures to emphasize important points. Appropriate gestures can enliven and animate what you say and help to communicate your enthusiasm and sincerity. If you do not move at all when you speak, others might perceive you as boring or tense.

4. Maintain good posture

Your posture is your body's position when you are sitting, standing, or walking. Posture communicates your mood, attitude, and interest in a topic. When communicating with others, sit or stand with an erect (but not stiff) posture, which sends a message of confidence and competence. Lean slightly towards your listeners to show you are receptive and interested in what they have to say. Avoid speaking when your back is turned or you are distracted with another task because this signals disinterest and insincerity.

QUICK TIP
Signs of discomfort in your listeners include looking away, stepping backwards, turning their body at an angle to you, or folding their arms over their chest.

5. Keep your distance

In communication, **proximity** is how physically close you are to your audience. Maintaining appropriate proximity is an important part of verbal communication. People expect you to respect their personal space and feel uncomfortable if you intrude on it. Appropriate proximity is affected by the relationship you have with the listener, the type of communication (intimate, friendly, professional, or public speaking), and your cultural norms. If you notice signs of discomfort that suggest you've moved into your listener's space, immediately increase the distance between you and your listener.

YOU TRY IT

Plan to use nonverbal cues when you speak. Open the VC1-Y3.docx document and follow the steps in the worksheet. When you are finished, submit the document to your instructor as requested.

FIGURE 1-3: Nonverbal language in the workplace

Pascal Luijpen/Photos.com

Gesture appropriately: This hand gesture seems aggressive

Hemera Technologies/Photos.com

Maintain eye contact: Lack of eye contact suggests conflict

Jupiterimages/Photos.com

Present pleasant facial expressions: A smile invites participation

Klaus Tiedge/Photos.com

Maintain good posture: An erect posture reinforces competence

TABLE 1-3: Nonverbal language do's and don'ts

element	do	don't
Eye contact	Maintain eye contact to foster trust and engagement	**Don't** avoid making eye contact with your listener or maintain prolonged contact
Facial expressions	Smile frequently and present a pleasant expression in general	**Don't** maintain a poker face
Gestures	Punctuate your speech with appropriate and meaningful gestures	**Don't** exaggerate or lose control of your gestures
Posture	Stand and sit with an erect posture to communicate confidence and competence	**Don't** turn your back to someone when speaking
Physical distance	Establish a proximity appropriate for your message and audience	**Don't** ignore signs that your listener is uncomfortable with your proximity

Learning the body language of success

More than the words you speak, your body language communicates the qualities that contribute to career success: confidence and leadership. In fact, the most successful business professionals use nonverbal communication that conveys authority and calm. Carmine Gallo, author of *10 Simple Secrets of the World's Greatest Business Communicators*, focuses on gestures and movement in body language. Instead of burning energy with nervous mannerisms such as drumming your fingers or rubbing your nose, Gallo recommends that you move with purpose. Videotape yourself for a few minutes as you give a presentation, and then watch for mannerisms that do not serve a useful purpose—they make you seem distracted or lacking control. However, standing too still as you speak makes you appear rigid and uncomfortable, especially if you have your hands in your pockets. If you are giving a presentation, Gallo suggests walking around the room. If you are having a conversation, take your hands out of your pockets so you can gesture naturally.

Source: Gallo, Carmine, "Actions Do Speak Louder Than Words," *BusinessWeek*, November 17, 2005.

Developing Credibility

Credibility is a perception that others have of your believability. Credibility is closely associated with trust, a crucial element in personal and professional relationships. Your audience is more attentive and attaches more significance to what you say if they believe you are a credible source of information. Although people do not automatically accept your ideas if they trust you, a lack of trust can undermine what you say. Table 1-4 summarizes the do's and don'ts of developing credibility. **case** Although you are fairly new to Quest Specialty Travel and the travel industry, you want to be sure your audience finds you credible at the career fair. You review the essential elements of a credible speaker.

ESSENTIAL ELEMENTS

1. Speak objectively and accurately

In the workplace, others make decisions based on the information you provide. To minimize the chances of making a bad decision, they consider your track record of accuracy and reliability. You can improve your credibility by speaking objectively, avoiding exaggerations or embellishments, and providing only accurate information. Back up your statements with verifiable facts and evidence, referring to notes, charts, or other documentation as shown in Figure 1-4.

QUICK TIP
One way to clarify an explanation is to answer who, what, when, where, why, and how questions about your topic.

2. Strive for clarity

The better your listeners understand your message, the more they accept it. Maximize your credibility by clearly and carefully expressing yourself. Encourage feedback from your audience by asking, "Can I clarify anything?" or "What do you think?" A typical communication error is to rush an explanation of something you plainly understand yourself. However, explaining your message improves everyone's comprehension of the topic. It also builds the trust listeners have in you and increases their commitment to the topic.

3. Coordinate your words and actions

Because your decisions, actions, and words send messages to your listener, be aware of how they work together. To be perceived as credible, the words you say should be consistent with your actions. If people note that your words and actions are inconsistent, they will have less faith in your messages or discount them entirely.

QUICK TIP
Empathy can also mean being patient and tolerant, especially when confronting potential conflicts.

4. Demonstrate empathy and concern

Credibility involves more than speaking clearly and honestly. People are more inclined to trust others who show concern and empathy—demonstrate that you understand their point of view. If you are trying to resolve a conflict, deliver disappointing news, or respond to a loss, for example, empathizing with your listeners enhances your credibility and makes them more receptive to your message.

5. Remember Aristotle's triangle

Aristotle analyzed effective speakers in ancient Greece and diagrammed their effectiveness in a triangle shown in Figure 1-5, which he called the **rhetorical triangle**. (*Rhetor* means "speaker" in Greek.) Aristotle taught that your speaking ability depends on how well you make three types of appeal to your audience: logical, ethical, and emotional appeals. As a speaker, this means you should consider three parts of communication to be successful: the subject, or what you have to say; yourself and your credibility; and your ability to empathize with your audience.

YOU TRY IT

Practice developing credibility by introducing a speaker to a group. Open the VC1-Y4.docx document and follow the steps in the worksheet. When you are finished, submit the document to your instructor as requested.

FIGURE 1-4: Speak objectively and accurately

Jupiterimages/Photos.com

FIGURE 1-5: Aristotle's triangle

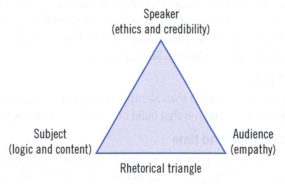

Speaker
(ethics and credibility)

Subject
(logic and content)

Audience
(empathy)

Rhetorical triangle

TABLE 1-4: Credibility do's and don'ts

element	do	don't
Objectivity	Speak objectively and provide factual evidence for your claims	Don't make biased or exaggerated statements
Clarity	Use familiar words and solicit feedback from your listeners	Don't rush an explanation or assume your listener already understands a topic
Consistency	Make your actions consistent with your words	Don't say one thing and do another
Empathy	Demonstrate you recognize your listener's point of view	Don't fail to show understanding, even if you disagree with your audience

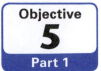

Giving and Receiving Feedback

Giving and receiving feedback is part of the communication process, and lets speakers know their listeners received and understood the message. As a speaker, you receive feedback about how others perceive you and your message. As a listener, you can improve communication by providing feedback such as nodding if you understand the message, paraphrasing to make sure you are interpreting the message correctly, and asking questions if you need more information. You also give feedback when others ask you to evaluate an idea, event, or document. Feedback in general should be positive, objective, and descriptive. Table 1-5 lists the do's and don'ts for giving feedback. **case** Juan Ramirez has also invited Anna McCloud, a new marketing assistant, to give a presentation to students at the career fair. You and Anna rehearse together and offer feedback to one another.

ESSENTIAL ELEMENTS

QUICK TIP

A good rule of thumb is to make two positive statements before offering a critical comment.

1. Emphasize the positive

To minimize defensiveness in your listener, include positive observations with your feedback. This lets the other person know you are being fair and have a balanced opinion of their performance. It also helps them listen to your message more constructively.

2. Use tact when providing feedback

Tact is the ability to act or speak in way that maintains good relations with others or avoids giving offense. When you provide feedback, consider what you are saying and how your listener is likely to receive it. Look for common ground, ask questions, and allow your colleague to make suggestions for improvement.

QUICK TIP

Feedback messages should describe a person's behavior, events, procedures, standards, and expectations.

3. Depersonalize negative messages

Instead of communicating a negative or critical message when you are charged with emotion, wait until you are calm and can look at the message objectively. Avoid making comments your audience might perceive as personal. Your objective is to fix problems and improve performance, not to assign blame. When offering critical feedback, avoid messages that include the word *you*. Instead, use the words *I* or *we* to express how you feel without attacking or blaming. See Figure 1-6.

4. Provide solutions

Focus on offering solutions rather than identifying problems or weaknesses. Constructive feedback includes recommendations and alternatives that build on your listener's strengths.

5. Choose your location and time

Consider where and when you approach someone to offer feedback—especially if the message is negative. Deliver feedback in a neutral, private location. See Figure 1-7. Do not confront someone in the presence of others, which could be publicly embarrassing. Choose a time that minimizes the interruption to your listener's day.

6. Give others permission to disagree with you

After you give feedback, be prepared to receive it. Listen to feedback with an open mind and learn what you can from it. Avoid interpreting disagreement or critical comments as personal attacks. Identify what you have in common, ask questions that seek solutions or alternatives, and look for a fair solution on which you can both agree.

YOU TRY IT

Practice giving feedback by offering suggestions to improve a presentation. Open the VC1-Y5.docx document and follow the steps in the worksheet. When you are finished, submit the document to your instructor as requested.

FIGURE 1-6: Examples of positive and negative feedback

Negative: You have a bad habit of fiddling with your hair during your presentation.	**Positive:** Walk around the room as you speak so that everyone can see and hear you.
"You" language: You didn't leave time for questions and never provided the Web address.	**"I" language:** I have a couple of questions and would like to know the Web address.
Blame-oriented: You let a potential customer just walk away.	**Solution-oriented:** How can we encourage people to sign up for a tour?

FIGURE 1-7: Choose your location and time

Sergei Butorin/Photos.com

TABLE 1-5: Feedback do's and don'ts

element	do	don't
Tone	• Express enthusiasm and appreciation • Praise efforts	• **Don't** sound skeptical or demanding • **Don't** avoid giving feedback at all
Language	• Identify your objective criteria • Conclude with a positive message • Focus on solutions and options, not personal qualities • Use "I" language	• **Don't** use too many negative words, such as *not*, *never*, and *bad* • **Don't** assign blame • **Don't** overlook solutions • **Don't** use "you" language
Tact	• Consider how your listener will receive your message • Listen actively and completely • Show understanding by asking questions and paraphrasing • Accept feedback from your listener	• **Don't** fail to show that you want to make improvements • **Don't** forget about how your listener interprets your body language
Setting	• Choose a private location • Look for a convenient time	• **Don't** interrupt your listener • **Don't** choose a time when the effects of a negative message might linger

Understanding the Basics of Verbal Communication

Objective 6 Part 1

Overcoming Barriers to Communication

Communication involves sending information that has meaning from one person or group to another. The communication process is only successful when the receiver understands the meaning of the information as the sender intends. Along the way, obstacles can prevent or disrupt communication. Be aware of these barriers so you can craft a message your audience is more likely to receive and understand. Table 1-6 summarizes the do's and don'ts of overcoming barriers to communication. [case] When you arrive at the career fair, you find that the room for your presentation is in a noisy, overheated location. You work with Juan and Anna to overcome these barriers.

ESSENTIAL ELEMENTS

QUICK TIP

Rehearse a presentation, speech, interview, or other important conversation and practice meaningful gestures instead of distracting habits.

1. Use appropriate language

Your choice of words significantly influences the quality of your communication. Using language that your audience can interpret in more than one way can lead to misunderstandings. Choose words that are familiar, unambiguous, and easily to understand. Provide concrete examples, if possible. Pay attention to your listener to make sure they understand the language you are using.

2. Make your messages clear

Communicate directly so that your messages are obvious and clear. Don't muddle your message by adding filler words that dilute what you are saying, such as *about*, *maybe*, and *a little bit*. See Figure 1-8. Choose words that make your messages clear and concise.

3. Send consistent signals

Your nonverbal communication should complement what you say. When the two differ, your listener believes your nonverbal cues and tends to ignore your words. Avoid distracting habits such as crossing your arms, putting your hands in your pockets, handling a cell phone, or turning away from people when you speak. Practice moving purposely instead.

QUICK TIP

Don't use impersonal communication media such as e-mail for sensitive messages.

4. Use the appropriate medium

Verbal media include face-to-face meetings, telephone calls, voice mail, and video conferences. Choose a medium that fits the message you are sending. For example, if you want to confirm an appointment, a voice mail message is appropriate. If you need to work out a decision, however, a face-to-face meeting is best. Consider the complexity of your message, the costs of a potential misunderstanding, your listener's ability to understand you, and the urgency of your message.

5. Reduce physical distractions

Physical distractions block or reduce effective communication. Examples include background noise, interruptions, uncomfortable temperatures, and busy environments. Reduce these physical distractions so you and your listener can concentrate on the conversation. If possible, close the door, turn off a cell phone, or suggest that you and your listener find a quieter place to chat.

YOU TRY IT

Identify barriers to communication and offer solutions. Open the VC1-Y6.docx document and follow the steps in the worksheet. When you are finished, submit the document to your instructor as requested.

FIGURE 1-8: Language that creates and avoids misunderstandings

Vague:	Clear:
The meeting will start about 10:00 a.m. tomorrow.	The meeting will start at 10:00 a.m. tomorrow.
You might mention a few more details about the meeting.	Do you have an agenda for the meeting?
Maybe you could help with setup beforehand.	Could you arrive ten minutes early to turn on the projector and distribute handouts?

TABLE 1-6: Overcoming barriers do's and don'ts

element	do	don't
Language	• Choose words that are familiar, unambiguous, and easy to interpret • Ask for feedback to make sure your listener understands	• **Don't** use filler words that can lead to misunderstandings • **Don't** use language your audience is unlikely to understand
Nonverbal signals	• Match your body language to your verbal language • Move with purpose	**Don't** distract your listeners by fidgeting or turning away
Media	Choose the medium that is right for your purpose and audience	**Don't** choose a medium that reduces the quality of the communication, such as a noisy cell phone
Physical distractions	Reduce physical distractions before you start to communicate	**Don't** ignore your listener's discomfort or put up with barriers such as a poor telephone connection

Voice mail etiquette

Voice mail is a medium for professional communication that can cause problems for the caller and the receiver. It is frustrating to leave a message and not receive a return call, or to call a company and get trapped in their voice mail system, unable to find an answer to a question. Following a few voice mail guidelines can help you avoid these problems. Be sure to record a personal greeting on your voice mail; don't rely on the standard mechanical greeting that was prerecorded on your phone. Include your name and department so callers know they have reached the correct number, and then direct callers to leave a message. Mention your normal work hours. If you have different hours temporarily, such as when you are on vacation, explain that so callers know they should not expect an immediate call back. Check your messages and return calls within 24 hours. Delete old messages to provide enough room for new ones. When you leave a voice mail message for someone, speak clearly and slowly. Include your name, phone number, and extension number, if necessary. Keep your message short, specific, and direct, and mention the best time to return your call.

Communicating Ethically

Ethics deals with principles for acceptable conduct, and usually refers to honest, fair behavior and decisions. It also involves the moral obligations you have to treat others as you want to be treated. Ethical and legal behaviors often overlap, though they are not the same. When communicating in professional and business situations, you need to carefully analyze your objectives, choices, and consequences to make a responsible and ethical decision. Table 1-7 summarizes the do's and don'ts for ethical communication. ▸ case After your presentation at the career fair, a friend of your family approaches you and reveals that he recently accepted a job managing Global Travel, Quest's major competitor. He mentions that he will reward you for any information about new tours Quest is developing. You want to maintain a friendly relationship and respond ethically.

1. Tell the truth

You can avoid many ethical dilemmas by speaking honestly. You don't need to divulge confidential information, or speak openly about sensitive or personal topics. However, avoid exaggerating your subjects, speaking in half-truths, or communicating with the intent to deceive your listener in any way. Your reputation is developed through your integrity, and honesty builds trust in business and personal relationships.

> **QUICK TIP**
> Include alternative solutions, consider other perspectives, and identify pros and cons when appropriate.

2. Present a balanced viewpoint

When discussing a topic or responding to a request for a recommendation or analysis, balance the pros and cons in your response to avoid bias. Presenting your listener with a single perspective provides incomplete or inaccurate information. Effective salespeople acknowledge the competition and overcome objections when persuading customers to try a new product or service. In general, you are perceived as a more trustworthy communicator if you discuss topics objectively and balance your response.

> **QUICK TIP**
> Introduce an opinion with a statement such as "I think," "I believe," or "it seems to me."

3. Separate fact from opinion

In the workplace, colleagues, managers, and customers depend on you to provide factual information they can use to make decisions. Be sure to clearly separate fact from opinion. A fact can be observed and independently verified. Your opinion is an idea or belief that you have. You might feel strongly about your opinion, but do not represent it as a fact.

4. Disclose information clearly

Some people mistakenly assume that disclosing an important detail briefly or in an inconvenient location, such as at the back of a report or buried in the fine print of a contract, is legally sufficient. However, this is an ethically questionable approach. If your listeners have a legitimate need to know something, you should present it in a clear, understandable, and appropriate format rather than making them read the fine print, as in Figure 1-9.

> **QUICK TIP**
> You can vary the amount of information that you disclose based on the other person's need to know.

5. Communicate the same message to everyone

When communicating with others, you might avoid conflict by adopting the popular perspective or saying what you think your listener wants to hear. However, doing so can compromise your integrity. Avoid sending different messages about a topic to different people. Assume that your listeners will compare notes and discover the inconsistencies.

Practice communicating ethically by responding to a situation that challenges your ethics. Open the **VC1-Y7.docx** document and follow the steps in the worksheet. When you are finished, submit the document to your instructor as requested.

FIGURE 1-9: Disclose information clearly

Franck Boston/Photos.com

TABLE 1-7: Ethical communication do's and don'ts

element	do	don't
Honesty	• Choose words that are familiar, unambiguous, and easy to interpret • Disclose all the information your listener needs to know to avoid misunderstandings and related problems	• **Don't** use language intended to deceive • **Don't** hide information that an audience has a right to know
Balance	Acknowledge the pros and cons of more than one point of view	**Don't** present a single point of view
Fact and opinion	Distinguish between verifiable facts and your opinions	**Don't** represent your opinion, however strong, as a fact
Consistency	Send the same basic message about a topic to all your listeners	**Don't** change your message to conform to what your listener wants to hear

Understanding Cross-Cultural Issues

As organizations expand internationally, you are more likely to work with others from different countries and cultures. When you do, be aware of your cultural influences and how they affect your communication. Doing so helps you recognize the cultural influences of your colleagues, customers, and suppliers. Estimates are that over 6,000 languages are spoken in various parts of the world. When you visit someone, respect differences in culture by following the expectations of the place. See Figure 1-10. Table 1-8 summarizes the do's and don'ts for cross-cultural communication. **case** The students and employers at the career fair have varied cultural backgrounds. As you meet and talk to people, you want to make sure your communication style is appropriate for your audience.

ESSENTIAL ELEMENTS

1. **Keep your messages simple**

   When speaking with people whose native language is different from yours, remember that they are managing two tasks at the same time. First, they are listening to and processing the language that you are speaking, which is not their native tongue. Second, they are trying to understand the message that you are communicating. You can help your listeners by keeping your messages simple and direct. Discuss one topic at a time and be sure your message is understood before changing topics.

   QUICK TIP
   Don't speak too loudly or slowly, however, or you risk offending your listener.

2. **Speak slowly and clearly**

   Although many people from other cultures speak and understand English, they might be accustomed to hearing it spoken with an accent different from yours. Help your listener by reducing your rate of speech, pausing occasionally, and articulating your words. Speak loudly enough to be heard easily.

   QUICK TIP
   Maintain eye contact when conversing with a nonnative speaker.

3. **Watch for signs of understanding**

   Many cultures consider it impolite to interrupt a speaker or ask someone to repeat what they've said. Instead, your listener might patiently listen without understanding as you speak. Look for expressions that indicate a lack of comprehension, such as a blank stare, forced smile, or confused looks. See Figure 1-11. Slow down, simplify your speech, and repeat your message.

   QUICK TIP
   Concentrate to understand what the speaker is saying and adjust to his or her pronunciation and accent.

4. **Listen carefully and uncritically**

   Show respect for others by listening attentively when they speak. Don't correct the grammar or pronunciation of nonnative speakers unless they ask for a correction. Avoid completing sentences or suggesting a word when they pause. Instead, provide positive nonverbal feedback such as nodding your head and smiling. If you don't understand what others are saying, wait until they are finished, and then ask questions about the topic rather than requesting that they repeat their words.

5. **Avoid clichés and idioms**

   A cliché is an expression that has been so overused, it communicates little information. An idiom is an expression that means something other than its literal meaning. People often use clichés and idioms as fillers in daily conversation. Avoid them when talking with a nonnative speaker.

YOU TRY IT

Practice understanding cross-culture issues by identifying communication problems in a conversation. Open the VC1-Y8.docx document and follow the steps in the worksheet. When you are finished, submit the document to your instructor as requested.

FIGURE 1-10: Respect differences in culture

Christopher Futcher/Photos.com

FIGURE 1-11: Watch for signs of misunderstanding

Hemera Technologies/Photos.com

Jacob Wackerhausen/Photos.com

TABLE 1-8: Cross-cultural do's and don'ts

element	do	don't
Message	Keep your message simple, clear, and familiar	Don't use clichés, idioms, or obscure language
Speaking pace	Speak slowly and clearly	Don't exaggerate the slow pace; speak naturally
Feedback	Be extra attentive to feedback that signals your listener does not understand your message	Don't wait for your listener to ask for explanations
Listening style	Listen patiently; you'll eventually catch on to the rhythms of an accent	Don't correct the grammar or pronunciation of a nonnative speaker

Technology @ Work: Web Conferencing

Web conferencing tools are software and services that let you use an Internet-connected computer to meet with others and communicate orally. Web conferences are similar to personal meetings because group members can share ideas and view the same material on a computer screen or whiteboard without physically traveling to the same location. Web meeting attendees can use microphones attached to their computers to speak or can use the telephone to connect to a conference call. Web conferences are especially useful for training and demonstrations. Popular Web conferencing software includes WebEx, GoToMeeting, and Microsoft Live Meeting. Figure 1-12 shows WebEx and Figure 1-13 shows GoToMeeting. **case** Juan Ramirez is considering holding a Web conference with the Quest Specialty Travel staff in New York. He asks you to investigate Web conferencing technology.

ESSENTIAL
ELEMENTS

QUICK TIP
Web conferencing software includes chatting or instant messaging features so meeting participants can ask questions without interrupting a speaker.

1. **Find a conference host**

   When setting up a Web conference, someone needs to act as the host. This is usually the person who is arranging the meeting. The host needs a subscription to a Web conference provider, a computer with an Internet connection, a Webcam or digital video camera for video (if necessary), and Web conferencing software to coordinate the meeting. If the host wants to show only software or a presentation on a computer, a video camera is not necessary.

2. **Reserve a time and invite participants**

   Web conference providers offer server space for your meeting, which you need to reserve ahead of time. You typically work with an event manager to register the meeting, reserve the server space, and set up the conference so that participants can connect successfully. The event manager usually provides the Web address and access codes to send to participants.

3. **Invite meeting participants**

   Determine who should attend the Web conference and use the conferencing software to invite them. Some software works with e-mail packages to send, schedule, and receive invitations. In the invitation messages, be sure to include the link and access code meeting attendees need to participate.

4. **Plan the visuals**

   Gather material for the meeting, including software, documents, and electronic presentations. Take advantage of the technology to enrich the discussion with video, images, slides, and shared applications. Create a welcome slide to display when participants first arrive so they know they are in the right place.

5. **Record the conference**

   Many Web conferencing services let you record the conference for people who can't attend. You can send them a digital video to watch at their convenience.

YOU TRY IT

Learn more about Web conferencing by working with Microsoft Live Meeting. Open the VC1-TechWork.docx document and follow the steps in the worksheet. When you are finished, submit the document to your instructor as requested.

FIGURE 1-12: WebEx

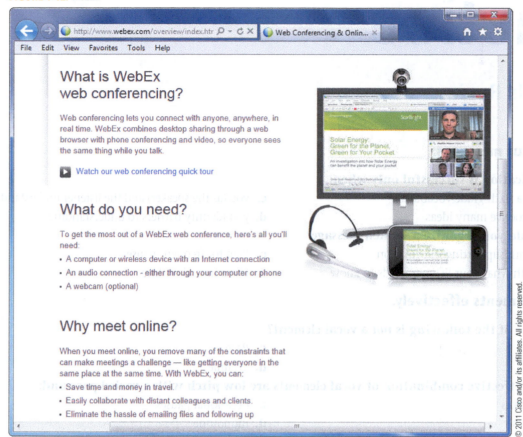

FIGURE 1-13: GoToMeeting

Verbal Communication

Practice

Soft Skills Review

Organize your messages.

1. **Communication is successful only when:**
   a. you use a sixth-grade vocabulary
   b. you introduce many ideas
   c. you (as the speaker) and the listener understand each other
   d. you identify barriers to understanding

2. **How should you organize a spoken message?**
   a. Begin with supporting information
   b. Start with what your listener needs to know
   c. Plan for frequent pauses
   d. Use a formal outline

Use vocal elements effectively.

1. **Which one of the following is *not* a vocal element?**
   a. Pitch
   b. Gesture
   c. Pace
   d. Volume

2. **The most effective combination of vocal elements are low pitch with a varied pace and:**
   a. lots of jokes
   b. no pauses
   c. occasional pauses
   d. monotone

Understand nonverbal language.

1. **Which one of the following is *not* a type of nonverbal cue?**
   a. Smiling
   b. Eye contact
   c. Speed of your voice
   d. Hand gestures

2. **What does proximity refer to in spoken communication?**
   a. Your listener's ability to interpret your words
   b. How physically close you are to your audience
   c. Your style of speaking
   d. Approximate meaning

Develop credibility.

1. **How can you improve your credibility when speaking?**
   a. Vary the pace and pitch of your voice
   b. Exaggerate and embellish
   c. Base conclusions on your opinions
   d. Speak objectively

2. **According to Aristotle, when speaking you should consider your subject, yourself, and your:**
   a. rhetor
   b. audience
   c. ethics
   d. background

Give and receive feedback.

1. **Which one of the following is *not* an effective way to give feedback?**
   a. Emphasize the positive
   b. Choose a private location
   c. Cross your arms
   d. Provide solutions

2. **When giving feedback, what should you focus on instead of identifying problems?**
   a. Assigning blame
   b. Solutions
   c. Body language
   d. Credibility

Overcome barriers to communication.

1. What types of words should you use to overcome barriers to communication?

   a. Foreign words

   b. Power words

   c. Ambiguous words

   d. Familiar words

2. Which of the following is *not* an appropriate medium for spoken communication?

   a. Presentation

   b. Phone call

   c. Face-to-face meeting

   d. Busy environment

Communicate ethically.

1. Ethics deals with:

   a. principles for acceptable conduct

   b. persuading customers

   c. complying with the law

   d. expressing opinions

2. Which of the following is *not* a way to communicate ethically?

   a. Say what your listener wants to hear

   b. Present a balanced point of view

   c. Be truthful

   d. Separate fact from opinion.

Understand cross-cultural issues.

1. When speaking to someone whose native language is different from yours, you should:

   a. correct grammar and pronunciation errors

   b. speak with animation and many gestures

   c. use the same accent as your listener

   d. discuss one topic at a time

2. An idiom is:

   a. a type of nonverbal communication

   b. an overused expression

   c. a dictionary definition

   d. an expression that means something other than its literal meaning

Technology @ work: Web conferencing.

1. Web conferencing tools are software and services that let you:

   a. organize presentations on the Web

   b. monitor Web sites

   c. use an Internet-connected computer to meet with others

   d. translate your spoken words to another language

2. What is the role of the Web conference host?

   a. To videotape the meeting

   b. To coordinate the meeting

   c. To launch the software

   d. To set up the Internet connections

Critical Thinking Questions

1. **You are interviewing for your dream job and the interviewer says the company is looking for someone with top-notch verbal skills. How do you answer?**

2. **Suppose you are discussing an important project with a colleague at your desk when a visiting supplier walks by and interrupts you by commenting on the way you are dressed. How do you respond?**

3. **Speaking and writing each have pros and cons as forms of communication. When should you use forms of oral communication? When should you use forms of written communication?**

4. **Do you think gossip has its place in the workplace? Should gossip be encouraged or discouraged by managers and other employees?**

5. **Many people in your company are being laid off, and you and other members of your department fear you might lose your jobs. You see a document on your supervisor's computer labeled "Staffing Plans." What do you do? Should you mention the document to your colleagues?**

Independent Challenge 1

You work as an administrative assistant at NorthStar, a four-season resort in eastern Maine. Kelly Mortensen is your supervisor, and she asks you to show a small group of businesspeople around the resort. They represent a business in Quebec that is considering whether to hold a conference at NorthStar. Before they arrive, you need to prepare the tour and plan what you will say. Part of the NorthStar resort is shown in Figure 1-14.

a. Open the **VC1-IC1.docx** document and follow the steps in the worksheet.

b. Proofread the document carefully to fix any grammar or formatting errors.

c. Submit the document to your instructor as requested.

FIGURE 1-14

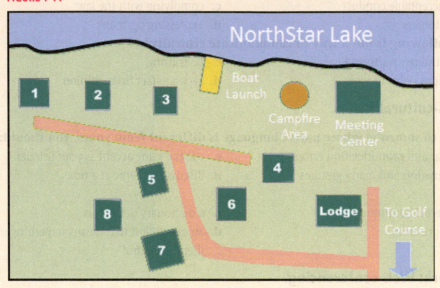

Independent Challenge 2

You work in the Bloomington Health Clinic, a family practice clinic in Bloomington, Indiana. Brad Diego manages the administrative staff, and is planning to hire a new receptionist to greet patients and schedule appointments. Brad organizes a team of interviewers, and asks you to participate.

a. Open the **VC1-IC2.docx** document and follow the steps in the worksheet.

b. Proofread the document carefully to fix any grammar or formatting errors.

c. Submit the document to your instructor as requested.

Real Life Independent Challenge

This Real Life Independent Challenge requires an Internet connection.

You have one more year before you need to start applying for a job. You decide to use this time to identify skills that employers want so you can make yourself as attractive as possible to a potential employer. Study the want ads online to identify the skills employers want.

a. Using a Web browser, visit the CareerBuilder Web site at *www.careerbuilder.com*.

b. Click the Select a Job Category arrow button, as shown in Figure 1-15, and then complete the following tasks on the CareerBuilder Web site:
- Select a category that appeals to you.
- Read the ads for jobs in that category.

c. In a word-processing document, list the qualities employers are seeking.

d. Choose three qualities and write about how you can improve your skills to meet their needs.

e. Proofread the document carefully to fix any grammar or formatting errors.

f. Submit the document to your instructor as requested.

FIGURE 1-15

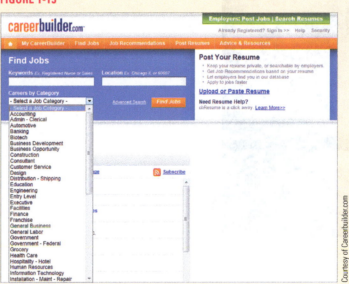

Courtesy of Careerbuilder.com

Team Challenge

This Team Challenge requires an Internet connection.

You work for the Global Village, an import/export company specializing in housewares made from sustainable materials. You and other members of the Marketing Department are preparing to accompany Louisa Chen, the company buyer, to Mexico and parts of Central America. Before you leave, Louisa asks your group to research nonverbal communication in Mexico, Costa Rica, and Guatemala. She is particularly interested in finding out how to dress appropriately.

a. Using your favorite search engine, search for information about nonverbal communication in Mexico and Central America. Look for explanations of hand gestures, practices for business meetings, and appropriate dress for professional meetings. Note the addresses of the Web sites that provide the most useful information.

b. In person or online, meet as a team to discuss your findings.

c. As a team, create a list of recommendations for Louisa about how to act and dress during the buying trip to Mexico and Central America.

d. Submit the list to your instructor as requested.

Be the Critic

Review the photo of a business meeting shown in Figure 1-16. These people are members of the Claims Department at an insurance company. The purpose of the meeting is to find ways to cut the budget of the Claims Department. Create an e-mail message that lists the nonverbal communication mistakes the participants might be making and offer specific suggestions for improvement. Send the critique to your instructor.

FIGURE 1-16

Jupiterimages/Photos.com

Working with Customers

Much of your professional life is likely to involve working with customers. A customer is the buyer or user of goods or services. In most businesses, the customer is the reason for being; without them, the business would not continue. Customers typically have a choice about who they do business with and prefer to work with people and organizations that best satisfy their needs. You can earn a customer's preference by developing your customer-service skills. Effective and empathetic communication is the basis of quality customer service, and helps you maintain successful relationships with customers. **case** You have just been promoted from administrative assistant in Human Resources to customer service representative in the Operations Department of Quest Specialty Travel. You now work with Nancy McDonald, who was recently named head of Customer Service. During your first week of training, Nancy wants you to become comfortable working with Quest customers and handling their requests and complaints.

OBJECTIVES

9   Understand customer service basics

10   Communicate empathetically

11   Ask questions to understand problems

12   Deny requests

13   Cope with angry customers

14   Deal with the unexpected

15   Work with customers with disabilities

Understanding Customer Service Basics

Successful customer or client service is the lifeblood of any business. An organization can offer promotions and discount their prices to attract new customers, but repeat business and ongoing relationships are the keys to profitability. **Customer service** refers to an organization's relationship with its customers: meeting their expectations, listening to their concerns, and solving their problems. Providing customer service involves communicating with customers, identifying their wants and needs, and developing customer-friendly procedures to serve them. Customers rate a company's service according to practical and personal factors. See Figure 2-1. Table 2-1 summarizes the basic customer service do's and don'ts. **case** Before you communicate directly with Quest customers, Nancy McDonald suggests you review the basics of providing customer service.

DETAILS

When providing service to customers, be sure to:

- **Communicate a professional image**

  Make your first contact with a customer businesslike and pleasant. Whether in person or on the phone, smile when you communicate with a customer, be enthusiastic and prompt, and use professional etiquette. Keep in mind that your primary goal is to promote goodwill for your company.

- **Listen to your customers**

  When serving customers, especially those with complaints, spend most of your time listening. **Active listening** means that you stop talking and concentrate on the customer's words, not on how to counter their arguments or respond to their claims. Active listening also helps you understand a customer's needs and the content of their messages. Listening shows that you value customers and respect what they have to say.

- **Ask questions**

  Make sure you understand explanations and requests by asking for clarification. You can also ask questions to gather all the facts you need to make a decision, to request suggestions for improvement, and to find out what your customers need and want. After you ask a question, be prepared to keep quiet while you listen to the response.

  > **QUICK TIP**
  > Ask questions with neutral wording to encourage feedback and clarify details.

- **Exceed expectations**

  One popular definition of excellent customer service is an organization's ability to consistently exceed customer expectations. You can do this by determining what a client wants, and then doing that and more. Being more attentive and helpful than your customers expect helps to build customer loyalty.

- **Provide service even without an immediate payoff**

  It is easy to pay attention to customers when you are trying to close a sale. However, the way you treat customers when no transaction is taking place creates a lasting impression. Look past the immediate payoff and take time to listen, answer questions, and solve problems, or help customers find someone who can.

- **Respond personally**

  When customers have a problem, they want to deal with a real person. However, your first reaction to a frustrated customer is probably avoidance. As a professional, you should overcome this reaction and deal directly with customers whenever possible. Call a disgruntled client instead of sending an e-mail message. Accept a phone call from a customer instead of transferring the call to voice mail. Step out from behind a desk, counter, or cash register when you speak with people. The personal contact shows you care and promotes problem solving.

FIGURE 2-1: Rating customer service

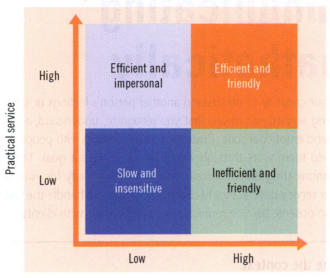

TABLE 2-1: Basic customer service do's and don'ts

communication role	do	don't
Sending messages	• Smile and show enthusiasm • Use professional etiquette • Promote goodwill	• Don't keep customers waiting to communicate with you • Don't reveal personal or emotional reactions
Listening	• Pay attention to content, not style, and try to understand the details • Control your responses and maintain a calm, professional demeanor • Wait for the customer to finish speaking • Encourage questions and additional comments • Use your body language to show you are actively involved	• Don't do anything else while listening • Don't assume you already know the customer's problem • Don't focus on exaggerations or misstatements • Don't become distracted by emotional words • Don't interrupt the customer
Responding	• Respond to complaints in person, on the phone, or with a personal note • Show you care and want to solve the problem	• Don't avoid contact with the customer • Don't hide behind impersonal language

Communicating Empathetically

Empathy is your capacity to understand another person's feelings or state of mind. When working with customers, being empathetic means that you recognize, understand, and respond appropriately to their needs, wants, and emotional state. Customers value working with people who can understand their point of view and help them work through a problem or achieve a goal. Table 2-2 summarizes the do's and don'ts of communicating empathetically. **case** You are ready for your first day at the Quest Specialty Travel customer service desk. Nancy McDonald volunteers to handle the first few phone calls and customer visits so you can observe her communicating empathetically with clients.

1. **Determine the context**

   Customers contact businesses for many reasons, such as to renew services, purchase additional products, answer questions, or complain about a problem they have. When talking to customers, listen to what they say to determine the purpose and context of their message. Observe how they deliver the message so you can be sensitive to their emotional state. Watch for signs suggesting they are angry, frustrated, confused, or distrustful. You need to understand the context of a speaker's words before you can empathize with them.

2. **Address your customer's emotions**

   If a customer's emotion is obvious, you can comment on it empathetically, especially if the customer is angry or dissatisfied. Statements such as, "You must have been disappointed when you received the wrong shipment," or "I can imagine that you were frustrated when the product didn't work properly," demonstrate that you understand the customer's reaction and are concerned about solving the problem.

3. **Put customers at ease**

   When talking to a customer who seems uncomfortable expressing anger or articulating a problem, put them at ease by validating their feelings. Do this with observations such as, "I know how upset I get when a company ships me the wrong product," or "It sounds like the delay created a lot of inconvenience for you."

4. **Acknowledge customer efforts**

   Customers often take steps to resolve a problem before contacting a company. Their actions might have been unsuccessful and contributed to their frustration. Even so, don't suggest that their steps were inappropriate, which listeners might interpret as demeaning. Instead, respectfully acknowledge the steps they performed and suggest an alternative solution.

5. **Use listener-centered language**

   To communicate with empathy, you must anticipate how your listener will decode what you say. Focusing on the listener with "you" language emphasizes how your message benefits them and clarifies the purpose of the message. Figure 2-2 shows examples of listener-centered language.

Practice communicating empathetically by responding to a customer complaint. Open the **VC2-Y10.docx** document and follow the steps in the worksheet. When you are finished, submit the document to your instructor as requested.

FIGURE 2-2: Listener-centered language

Speaker focused:
Our policy is to issue refunds up to two weeks before a trip.

Listener focused:
You can receive a refund if you cancel a reservation up to two weeks before the trip.

"I/we" point of view:
We must receive online verification before we can ship the tickets via overnight delivery.

"You" point of view:
Please verify your reservation online so you can receive tickets the next day.

Unclear purpose:
The Legal Department has a passport policy that complies with federal policy, which you must follow before traveling outside U.S. borders.

Clear purpose:
If you are traveling outside the U.S., check the federal passport policy for your destination—you might need to travel with your passport.

TABLE 2-2: Communicating empathetically do's and don'ts

element	do	don't
Context	• Listen to the content of a message to determine its purpose • Listen to how the message is delivered to determine its emotional context • Comment on a customer's emotional state using neutral language • Put listeners at ease by validating their reactions	• Don't ignore signs that a speaker is angry, frustrated, or disappointed • Don't comment on a customer's emotional state using emotional language
Acknowledging	• Ask questions to find out what customers did to resolve a problem • Acknowledge these efforts • Offer alternatives • Anticipate how your listener will respond to your message • Adopt the listener's point of view • Use "you" language	• Don't suggest that steps customers took to resolve a problem were inappropriate • Don't acknowledge the problem using impersonal or "I/we" language

Verbal Communication

Asking Questions to Understand Problems

Asking questions helps you listen carefully, clarify messages, encourage customer communication, and resolve problems. Effective questioning means knowing which questions to ask, when to ask them, and how to phrase them. Recall that part of customer service involves meeting customer expectations, identifying their wants and needs, and solving their problems. The most direct way to learn about a customer's expectations, desires, and problems is to ask questions and listen carefully to the answers. Two-way conversations build relationships because they help develop mutual awareness and trust. Table 2-3 summarizes the do's and don'ts for asking questions. **case** When you answer the phone at the Quest customer service desk, a customer reports he is dissatisfied with the preparations for a tour and wants to cancel his reservation. As Nancy McDonald suggested, you respond by asking a series of questions.

ESSENTIAL ELEMENTS

QUICK TIP

Monitor the number of questions you ask and your tone—you don't want to interrogate your customers.

1. Ask the appropriate type of question

You can ask at least four types of questions, as shown in Figure 2-3. **Open-ended questions** do not have a particular answer. Ask open-ended questions to encourage the other person to articulate motivations, ideas, and solutions. **Closed questions** are specific and concrete, and generally seek a "yes" or "no" answer. Ask a closed question when you need a direct answer. Ask **follow-up questions** in response to an answer that your customer provides. Design these questions to discover more information or learn an opinion. Asking follow-up questions also shows that you are listening carefully and thinking about what the other person says. Ask **feedback questions** about the conversation or problem-solving process itself to determine what is important to the customer. Feedback questions help you gauge your customer's satisfaction with the steps that you are taking and the solution you proposed.

2. Establish rapport

When a customer contacts you regarding a problem, show genuine interest in their situation. Ask questions to learn about the details of their complaint—the who, what, where, when, and how facts. Summarize their responses and ask follow-up questions such as "Is that correct?" Taking time to understand the details establishes rapport and trust, and helps you identify possible solutions.

3. Clarify understanding

Frustrated customers are often too distracted to listen actively and focus instead on what they want to say. Ask open-ended and follow-up questions that encourage customers to explain why they are contacting you and to define their request or problem clearly. Paraphrase their answers to verify your understanding. See Figure 2-4.

QUICK TIP

Be sure to give credit to the other person when they find an answer.

4. Motivate the customer

People contacting customer service to resolve a problem might be more interested in offering, not accepting, comments and ideas. When working with an upset customer, avoid competing for the best idea or debating the facts. Instead, ask questions to solicit solutions. If customers discover the answer to their problem, they will own and accept the solution.

YOU TRY IT

Practice asking questions to understand problems by resolving a customer's problem. Open the **VC2-Y11.docx** document and follow the steps in the worksheet. When you are finished, submit the document to your instructor as requested.

FIGURE 2-3: Types of questions

Open-ended
What do you suggest?

How would you like to resolve the problem?

How do you generally use the product?

Closed
Do you have a copy of the itinerary?

Have you contacted customer service before?

Is this the first problem you've had with Quest Specialty Travel?

Follow-up
Can you give me an example of bad service at the hotel?

What happened after you missed the tour bus?

Feedback
Would you be satisfied with a partial refund?

Can I send you a new copy of the tour schedule?

FIGURE 2-4: Ask questions to understand customer problems

Jupiterimages/Photos.com

TABLE 2-3: Question do's and don'ts

question type	do	don't
Open-ended	Encourage the other person to articulate motivations, ideas, and solutions	**Don't** stray from the main topic of the questions
Closed	Ask "yes" and "no" questions to find facts and details	**Don't** ask too many questions, or you'll sound as if you're cross-examining your customer
Follow-up	Paraphrase to make sure you understand the message	**Don't** pretend to understand
Feedback	Discover what is important to the customer and whether they are satisfied	**Don't** compete with a customer for the best idea

Denying Requests

When a customer makes a specific request, you sometimes have to deny it. Some companies train their employees to avoid the word "no" when dealing with customers to prevent disappointing them. However, your goal should be to make sure the customer understands and acknowledges the negative message—people can accept a denial if they understand the reasons for it. Customers also want to know that you are taking their request seriously. When denying a request directly, conveying empathy helps to foster or maintain the customer's goodwill toward your organization. Taking an indirect approach, however, is more likely to enhance a professional relationship. Figure 2-5 outlines the steps for denying a request. `case` A client scheduled to depart on an adventure tour of Scotland in a week arrives at the customer service desk, requesting that you transfer her reservation to a later tour in the summer. However, the deadline for transfers has passed, and you must deny her request.

ESSENTIAL ELEMENTS

1. **Rephrase the request**

   Instead of turning down a customer directly, first demonstrate that you fully understand the request or question. Rephrase the request and ask the customer to verify it. If customers think you don't understand, they often escalate the matter. Figure 2-6 shows examples of language to use when denying requests.

   QUICK TIP

   Besides "no" and "not," negative words include "unwilling," "impossible," "never," and "reject."

2. **Explain the reasons**

   Without using negative words, explain why you have to refuse a customer's request. Although customers resent explanations based on rules and policies, such as, "It's company policy to transfer overseas reservations only up to one month before the departure date," they do appreciate explanations about the reasons behind the rules. See Figure 2-6. Offering reasons demonstrates that you care about your customers, whereas saying "no" without an explanation makes your decision seem inflexible.

3. **Tell them what you can do**

   When you must deny a request, soften the refusal by offering an alternative, if possible. People appreciate having a choice, and usually perceive your offer as an effort to help. Conclude your communication by telling the customer what you can do for them instead of what you can't do.

4. **Try turning a "no" into a "yes"**

   Sometimes, by being flexible and creative, you can find a way to satisfy the customer without causing business problems. Show that you are willing to work with customers to achieve their goals. Find a creative workaround that solves the customer's problem without creating new ones for your company. See Figure 2-7.

   QUICK TIP

   A mixed message leads to misunderstanding and frustration.

5. **Be aware of your nonverbal communication**

   When you deny a request in person, your posture and facial gestures should send the same message that your words do. Use a polite but firm tone of voice, stand erect, and look the other person in the eye when speaking. Avoid defensive postures such as crossing your arms or retreating behind a desk.

YOU TRY IT

Practice denying requests by responding to a customer's telephone request. Open the VC2-Y12.docx document and follow the steps in the worksheet. When you are finished, submit the document to your instructor as requested.

FIGURE 2-5: Steps for denying a request

Rephrase	Explain	Refuse
• Restate the request • Ask for verification	• Provide reasons • Use positive language	• Soften the refusal • Provide an alternative • Offer a creative solution

FIGURE 2-6: Explain the reasons

Rephrase the request:
"You want to transfer your reservation to the August tour. Is that correct?"

Tell them what you can do:
"Although I cannot transfer your reservation now, I can refund the cost of the trip except for deposits."

Explain the reasons:
"We have already made many arrangements for you in Scotland, and it's too late to change those reservations."

Turn "no" into "yes":
"Instead of changing your reservation, we could transfer it to a friend or family member, and then you could reschedule in August."

FIGURE 2-7: Try turning a "no" into a "yes"

Jacob Wackerhausen/Photos.com

Customer service representatives

If you work as a customer service representative, you are a direct contact for customers. You respond to questions about products or services and handle and resolve complaints by phone, e-mail, fax, regular mail, or in person. You often work in a call center and use computers to access and update customer information. Some customer questions are routine, such as those inquiring about the balance on a bill or requesting printed information about products and services. Other

questions are more complex and can involve helping customers make purchasing decisions or complete a transaction. When you receive a customer complaint, you usually need to resolve it according to company guidelines. For example, you might need to ask a series of questions to determine the details of the complaint or receive authorization before offering refunds or exchanges.

Verbal Communication

Coping with Angry Customers

At some point in your career, you will confront an angry customer, especially if you deal directly with the public. The customer might be angry because your company failed to meet their expectations, made an error, or otherwise caused problems for them. You need to address the problem immediately and defuse their anger. Table 2-4 lists the do's and don'ts for coping with angry customers. **case** Nancy McDonald has been observing you during your first week of customer service training, and says you are ready to perform a difficult service task—handling an angry customer. She has one on hold and asks you to take the call.

ESSENTIAL ELEMENTS

QUICK TIP
Be sure to respond as soon as possible to show you care about the customer.

1. Remember why they are upset

Working with an angry customer is not a pleasant task and can be intimidating. Fortunately, angry customers are rarely upset with you personally. They might be frustrated because they are not getting what they want or need from your company and cannot solve the problem themselves. They could also be disappointed by a failure or deficiency in your company's products or services. Realizing that their reaction is legitimate helps you to see past the anger and act professionally.

QUICK TIP
If others are present, suggest moving the discussion to where you won't be disturbed.

2. Avoid an audience

If an angry customer confronts you in a public area, the presence of others can complicate your conversation. Some angry people are encouraged by the attention of an audience or are further frustrated by obstacles they create. Try to avoid other people and work directly with the customer in a quiet place.

3. Stay calm and neutral

As a means of self-preservation, you react physically to anger with a "fight or flight" reflex. This is why most people avoid conflict and delivering bad news—they fear an angry reaction. Others have a tendency to fight back. Both responses are counterproductive because they do not solve the underlying problem. Take time to make sure you are calm, control the pitch and rate of your voice, and speak with composure, using neutral language as you talk to an angry customer. See Figure 2-8.

QUICK TIP
A sincere apology and a promise to help are the quickest ways to calm an angry customer.

4. Apologize

Apologies are powerful tools that can quickly reduce anger. Apologize to express regret, but avoid accepting responsibility if doing so could create legal problems. Instead of accepting responsibility, you can acknowledge the problem with comments such as, "I am sorry that you are having this problem. How may I help you?" or "I am sorry that this doesn't work the way that you want it to."

5. Explain how you will help

Your customer is approaching you because they want to solve a problem. What they most want to know is that you will help them or connect them with someone who can. Clearly communicate that you will help them solve their problem before you ask questions or start troubleshooting.

6. Conclude with a thank you

Leave the customer with a positive impression of you and your organization by thanking them for the chance to help with their problem. Figure 2-9 outlines a successful conversation with an angry customer.

YOU TRY IT

Practice coping with angry customers by describing how you would react in a customer service scenario. Open the **VC2-Y13.docx** document and follow the steps in the worksheet. When you are finished, submit the document to your instructor as requested.

FIGURE 2-8: Stay calm when talking to an angry customer

Jupiterimages/Photos.com

FIGURE 2-9: Conversation with an angry customer

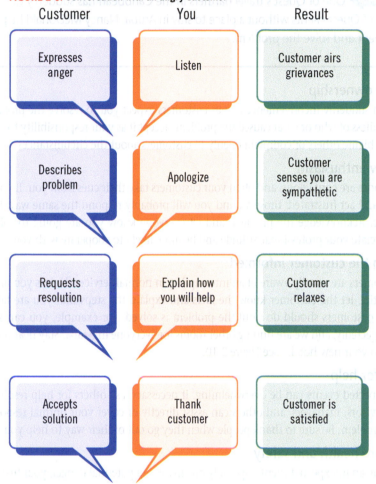

Customer	You	Result
Expresses anger	Listen	Customer airs grievances
Describes problem	Apologize	Customer senses you are sympathetic
Requests resolution	Explain how you will help	Customer relaxes
Accepts solution	Thank customer	Customer is satisfied

TABLE 2-4: Handling anger do's and don'ts

element	do	don't
Reaction	• Respond as soon as possible • Focus on the objective reasons for the customer's anger • Choose a setting where you can listen to the customer	• Don't take the anger personally • Don't talk to the customer in a public or noisy place
Apology	• Express regret • Explain what you will do to prevent a recurrence	• Don't admit responsibility if it might be grounds for a lawsuit • Don't offer a standard, impersonal apology
Conclusion	• Explain how you will help • Connect the customer to someone who can help • Demonstrate that you take their concern seriously	• Don't minimize the customer's problem, even if it is common • Don't forget to thank the customer

Dealing with the Unexpected

Plans aren't always carried out as expected. Shipments are delayed, a product is defective, or the store-room runs out of stock. Because scenarios such as these are common in business, anticipate problems and unexpected obstacles, and develop backup plans if possible. Unexpected problems in particular lead to frustration and disappointment. Although you cannot foresee every possible problem, follow some basic guidelines to deal with unexpected events. Table 2-5 lists the do's and don'ts for dealing with the unexpected. **case** One of Quest's travel partners in the Caribbean has suddenly gone out of business, leaving hundreds of Quest clients without a place to stay in Aruba. Nancy McDonald helps you confront this unexpected event and solve the problem.

1. Take ownership

When suddenly inconvenienced, your customers expect you to resolve the problem as quickly as possible. Regardless of who or what caused the problem, accept it as your responsibility to correct it. As a professional, don't blame others or complain openly to customers about the circumstances.

2. Show enthusiasm

Attitudes are contagious, and often your customers take their cues from you. If you are caught off guard and look and act frustrated, those around you will probably respond the same way. Instead, smile and be optimistic. Acknowledge the problem, and let everyone know you are going to solve it. Your customers will appreciate your professional attitude and be more likely to cooperate with you.

3. Keep the customer informed

Customers are usually aware of an interruption in normal services. Unless you must keep the problem confidential, let the customer know the facts and explain the steps that you are taking to resolve it. Explain what customers should do until the problem is solved. For example, you can say, "The hotel has closed unexpectedly, and we are finding other rooms for everyone in Aruba. Stay near the dock so we can transport you to your new hotel." See Figure 2-10.

4. Ask for help

Unexpected events can be overwhelming. If necessary, ask others for help resolving problems. Coworkers, supervisors, managers, and others can assist directly or cover your normal responsibilities while you solve the problem. Be sure to thank people when they go out of their way to help you.

5. Ensure health and safety

During an unexpected event, especially one involving potential danger, your first obligation is to ensure the health and safety of yourself, your customers, and those around you. Follow your organization's emergency procedures, call for the appropriate authorities, and look to the needs of others.

Practice dealing with the unexpected by resolving a surprise problem. Open the VC2-Y14.docx document and follow the steps in the worksheet. When you are finished, submit the document to your instructor as requested.

FIGURE 2-10: Keep customers informed

vm/Photos.com

TABLE 2-5: Dealing with the unexpected do's and don'ts

element	do	don't
Responsibility	Take responsibility for the problem no matter who or what caused it	**Don't** complain or blame others
Enthusiasm	• Acknowledge the problem • Show enthusiasm about solving it	• **Don't** reveal your frustration or fatigue • **Don't** stop brainstorming ways to solve the problem
Conclusion	• Explain how you will help • Connect the customer to someone who can help • Demonstrate that you take the customer's concerns seriously	• **Don't** minimize the customer's problem, even if it is common • **Don't** forget to thank the customer

Working with Customers with Disabilities

A disability is the lack of physical or mental ability relative to a standard or norm. Impairment is a condition that falls short of disability, but still affects people in some way. According to the U.S. Bureau of the Census, over 50 million Americans have disabilities or impairments, so you are likely to work with customers who have one or the other. ▶case◀ A customer calls and reports that she is organizing a group of travelers in wheelchairs and wants to meet with you to discuss accessible travel. You arrange the meeting, and talk to Nancy McDonald about guidelines Quest offers for serving customers with disabilities.

ESSENTIAL ELEMENTS

1. **Maintain eye contact**

   Look directly at any person with a disability when talking, even if the person has an interpreter or companion present. When having a conversation with someone in a wheelchair, try to sit at eye level with the person. You will both feel more comfortable and communicate more freely. See Figure 2-11.

2. **Speak slowly and clearly**

   Speak calmly, slowly, and distinctly to people who have hearing problems or difficulty understanding. Stand directly in front of the person and use gestures to help you communicate. Allow people with speech impairments to finish what they are saying. Don't talk for them, complete their sentences, or interrupt. Ask questions that permit short answers or a nod of the head.

3. **Let them set the pace**

   When walking with a person who is physically or visually impaired, allow them to set the pace. If the person asks for or accepts your offer of help, don't reach for their arm or hand. Extend your arm instead and let them take hold of you. Be careful about talking while you walk. Some people have difficulty breathing or need to concentrate on their movement rather than chatting with you.

4. **Always ask first**

   Ask people with disabilities if they need or want help before trying to assist them. If they want assistance, ask for specific instructions on how you can be helpful. Don't push a wheelchair without first asking the occupant's permission. Don't take offense if the other person rejects your offer of assistance.

> **QUICK TIP**
> To use bias-free language consistently, avoid messages that exclude, stereotype, or offend others.

5. **Use appropriate language**

   The guiding principle for unbiased language is to maintain the integrity of individuals as whole people by avoiding language that implies that a person as a whole is disabled (such as "a disabled person"); equates people with their condition (such as "epileptics"); has negative overtones (such as "stroke victim"); or is regarded as a slur (such as "gimp" or "cripple").

YOU TRY IT

Practice working with customers with disabilities by revising a conversation. Open the VC2-Y15.docx document and follow the steps in the worksheet. When you are finished, submit the document to your instructor as requested.

FIGURE 2-11: Sit down to maintain eye contact with customers in wheelchairs

Digital Vision/Photos.com

Telephone etiquette when talking to customers with disabilities

In January 2009, the Americans with Disabilities Amendments Act went into effect, expanding opportunities for the 56 million Americans with disabilities. The act amends the original 1990 law to recognize more disabilities that affect "one or more major life activity," such as learning disorders and other cognitive impairments. Even without the law, serving customers with disabilities makes good business sense. Considering that one in five Americans has a disability, they form a $200 billion market of potential consumers. This growing market needs customer service just as any other market does. Because most customer service conversations take place on the phone, you should be aware of special etiquette guidelines that apply when you are talking to customers with disabilities on the telephone. When conversing with someone who has voice impairments, listen attentively and avoid speaking for the customer or finishing sentences. You might need to adjust the volume, quality, or frequency of the audio on the phone to make their voice clearer. People with fine motor impairments might have limited use of their hands or fingers, so allow extra time for these customers to take notes or use a keyboard. If a customer has a cognitive impairment, be patient about offering an explanation more than once. Take time to understand the customer and make sure the customer understands you. In general, treat the customer with respect and courtesy, listen actively, and offer assistance as necessary.

Technology @ Work: Internet Monitoring

To learn more about their customers, many companies monitor the Internet for activities and comments related to their products and services. To do so, they use tools such as Google Alerts, shown in Figures 2-12 and 2-13. Other **Internet monitoring tools** work in a similar way, such as TweetLater, which monitors Twitter comments; Backtype, which monitors social networking sites; and SM2, which is designed for larger businesses. If you work in sales, marketing, or customer service, you can set up keywords or topics you want Google Alerts to track, such as the name of your product or company. Google Alerts then monitors the entire Web and sends the results of what it finds to you by e-mail. The results are links to Web pages, blogs, online articles, videos, and reviews, for example, that mention your company. If customers comment about your products, you can contact them to show appreciation or offer to solve their problem. This proactive approach is proving popular with consumers, who are often frustrated when trying to contact customer service representatives in large companies. **case** Nancy McDonald is eager to improve the customer service at Quest Specialty Travel and wants to know more about Internet monitoring tools such as Google Alerts. She asks you to find out how to set up and use a Google Alert.

ESSENTIAL ELEMENTS

1. **Visit the Google Alerts home page**

   Open your Web browser and go to *www.google.com/alerts*. Enter one or more keywords for the alert you want to set up. For example, to track Web content that mentions your company, enter your company's name.

2. **Select the type of alert you want to receive**

   You can choose one of six types of alerts: Everything, which tracks news articles, Web sites, and blogs; News, which tracks the latest news articles; Blogs, which tracks the latest blog posts; Video, which monitors the latest online videos; Discussion, which tracks discussions in Google Groups; and Books, which tracks content in Google Books.

3. **Select a frequency**

   Choose how often you want to receive the alerts. You can receive them as soon as Google Alerts finds a match to your keyword, once a day, or once a week.

4. **Provide an e-mail address**

   Enter the e-mail address where you want to receive the Google Alerts.

5. **Finish creating the alert**

   Click the Create Alert button, shown in Figure 2-12. Google Alerts will verify your e-mail address and then send you updated alerts according to the frequency you selected.

6. **Manage your alerts**

   Revise your alert settings on the Manage Alerts page, shown in Figure 2-13, if you are receiving too much or too little information.

YOU TRY IT

Learn more about Internet monitoring by setting up a Google Alert. Open the VC2-TechWork.docx document and follow the steps in the worksheet. When you are finished, submit the document to your instructor as requested.

FIGURE 2-12: Setting up a Google alert

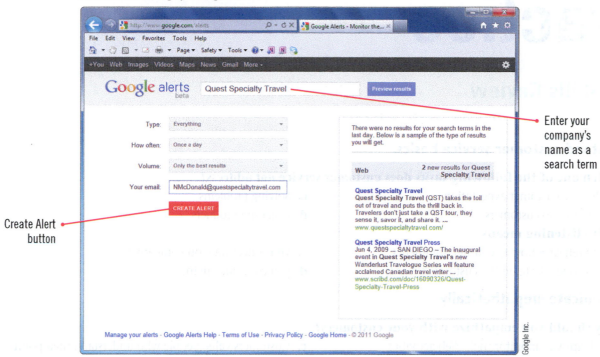

Enter your company's name as a search term

Create Alert button

FIGURE 2-13: Managing Google alerts

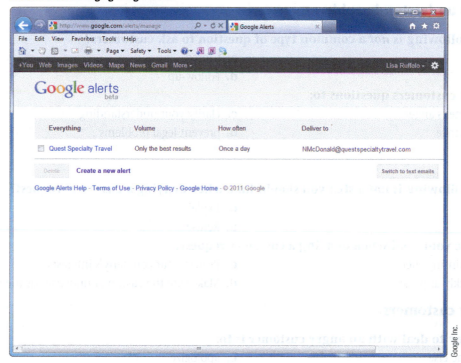

Practice

Soft Skills Review

Understand customer service basics.

1. **Which one of the following tasks does customer service *not* address?**
   - **a.** Meeting customer expectations
   - **b.** Listening to customers
   - **c.** Solving problems
   - **d.** Updating products

2. **Active listening means:**
   - **a.** you rehearse how to counter arguments
   - **b.** you concentrate on the customer's words
   - **c.** you concentrate on company policy
   - **d.** you continue talking

Communicate empathetically.

1. **Why should you empathize with your customers?**
   - **a.** It helps you monitor their Web activities
   - **b.** It helps you distract them with emotional words
   - **c.** Customers value people who understand their point of view
   - **d.** Customers appreciate impersonal language

2. **What kind of language should you use to empathize with your customers?**
   - **a.** "You" language
   - **b.** "I/we" language
   - **c.** Emotional language
   - **d.** Opinionated language

Ask questions to understand problems.

1. **Which of the following is *not* a common type of question to ask customers?**
   - **a.** Ethical
   - **b.** Open-ended
   - **c.** Closed
   - **d.** Follow-up

2. **You should ask customers questions to:**
   - **a.** avoid a customer's anger
   - **b.** keep your distance
   - **c.** clarify your understanding
   - **d.** prevent legal problems

Deny requests.

1. **Which of the following is *not* a step you should take when denying a customer request?**
   - **a.** Rephrase
   - **b.** Control
   - **c.** Explain
   - **d.** Refuse

2. **What should be your goal when denying a customer request?**
   - **a.** Avoid disappointing them
   - **b.** Say no as quickly as possible
   - **c.** Protect your company's interests
   - **d.** Make sure the customer understands the reasons

Cope with angry customers.

1. **An effective way to deal with an angry customer is to:**
   - **a.** blame someone else
   - **b.** express anger yourself
   - **c.** apologize
   - **d.** walk away until the customer is calm

2. **How should you conclude a conversation with an angry customer?**
   - **a.** Minimize their problem
   - **b.** Explain how you will help
   - **c.** Ask open-ended questions
   - **d.** Make small talk

Deal with the unexpected.

1. **What can you do when an unexpected event causes problems for a customer?**
   - **a.** Identify who is at fault
   - **b.** Call a lawyer
   - **c.** Accept responsibility
   - **d.** Avoid talking to customers if they are upset

2. **During an unexpected event, your first obligation is to:**
   - **a.** ensure the health and safety of those involved
   - **b.** prevent customers from getting angry
   - **c.** inform your colleagues
   - **d.** explain company policy

Work with customers with disabilities.

1. **When working with customers who have disabilities, you should:**
   - **a.** take care of everything yourself
   - **b.** remain aloof
   - **c.** ask if they need or want help
   - **d.** finish their sentences

2. **How can you use bias-free language consistently?**
   - **a.** Refrain from personal topics
   - **b.** Avoid messages that exclude, stereotype, or offend others
   - **c.** Use "I/we" language
   - **d.** Find the latest terminology on the Web

Technology @ work: Internet monitoring.

1. **Why do companies use Internet monitoring tools?**
   - **a.** To prevent employees from using the Web
   - **b.** To learn how to listen actively
   - **c.** To learn more about their customers
   - **d.** To learn how to search the Web

2. **Which of the following alerts does Google Alerts *not* offer?**
   - **a.** Blogs
   - **b.** News
   - **c.** Weather
   - **d.** Video

Critical Thinking Questions

1. You are working in a customer service call center and handling an irate customer who is upset about a mistake you made. How should you deal with the customer?

2. Suppose you are helping to solve a customer's problem with your company's product, and discover the customer has been misled about what the product can do. What do you say to the customer?

3. Your lifelong goal is to be a scriptwriter, but in the meantime, you are looking for a low-key job with plenty of time to let you write. Someone suggests you try customer service. Should you pursue a customer service job?

4. A customer contacts you, wanting a full refund for a product that was shipped late and to the wrong address. How do you respond?

5. Your manager has been using Internet monitoring tools and doesn't like what customers are saying about your company's products. She encourages you to post comments on blogs that are more favorable. To protect your confidentiality, she suggests you do so using a fictitious screen name. How do you handle this request?

Independent Challenge 1

You work in the Customer Service Department at NorthStar, a four-season resort in eastern Maine. Kelly Mortensen, a supervisor at the resort, asks you to talk to a pair of disgruntled customers. They are disappointed with their accommodations and feel they are being overcharged. The room is shown in Figure 2-14.

FIGURE 2-14

Ken Rygh/Photos.com

a. Open the **VC2-IC1.docx** document and follow the steps in the worksheet.

b. Proofread the document carefully to fix any grammar or formatting errors.

c. Submit the document to your instructor as requested.

Independent Challenge 2

You work in the Bloomington Health Clinic, a family practice clinic in Bloomington, Indiana. As a patient service representative, you talk to patients and help solve their problems. The mayor of Bloomington is a new patient at the clinic, and requests Dr. Driscoll as his personal physician. However, the clinic's policy is to assign new patients to physicians who have a light patient load. Dr. Driscoll's patient roster is full.

a. Open the **VC2-IC2.docx** document and follow the steps in the worksheet.

b. Proofread the document carefully to fix any grammar or formatting errors.

c. Submit the document to your instructor as requested.

Real Life Independent Challenge

This Real Life Independent Challenge requires an Internet connection.

You are preparing for a job search and want to enhance your skills so they are as appealing as possible to a potential employer. One skill that employers value is listening, though it is not often taught in formal classes. You can develop your listening skills through observation, study, and practice.

Real Life Independent Challenge (continued)

a. Using your favorite search engine, search for tips on active listening.

b. Also search for particular listening skills people in your chosen field of study need to develop.

c. Observe the people around you and note their listening behavior. Develop a list of active listening techniques and postures, such as those shown in Figure 2-15 and Figure 2-16, and listening behavior to avoid.

FIGURE 2-15

Jupiterimages/Photos.com

FIGURE 2-16

Catherine Yeulet/Photos.com

Verbal Communication

d. In a word-processing document, list the listening behaviors you want to adopt and those you want to avoid.

e. Proofread the document carefully to fix any grammar or formatting errors.

f. Submit the document to your instructor as requested.

Team Challenge

You work for the Global Village, an import/export company specializing in products made from sustainable materials. A new restaurant chain has placed a large order for placemats, napkins, and other textiles from Guatemala, but they have not arrived at the Global Village warehouse. Louisa Chen, the buyer for Global Village, calls to say the Guatemalan company did not pack the textiles in time to ship them to your warehouse. As a result, the restaurant chain cannot furnish its new restaurants.

a. Meet as a team to discuss possible solutions to Global Village's problem.

b. Discuss the role of the following people to solve the problem: you as a customer service representative, Louisa Chen, the owner of the restaurant chain, and the warehouse supervisor.

c. As a team, create a list of recommendations for handling the problem. Be sure to discuss how to discuss the problem with the Guatemalan supplier and the restaurant chain.

d. Submit the list to your instructor as requested.

Be the Critic

Review the conversation shown in Figure 2-17 between a customer service representative at an electronics company and a customer making a request. Analyze the conversation, noting its weaknesses, and send a list of the weaknesses to your instructor.

FIGURE 2-17

Customer: I purchased a professional-quality camera at your store, and have not been able to take a single photo with it.

Customer service representative: Can I have your name and phone number?

Customer: Excuse me? [Gives name and phone number.]

Customer service representative: Did you purchase an extended warranty contract?

Customer: For the camera? No, I did not.

Customer service representative: That's too bad. It would take care of your problem.

Customer: A warranty can't teach me how to use a camera.

Customer service representative: We don't offer training with our cameras.

Customer: I don't want training. I want to exchange the camera for one that's easier to use.

Customer service representative: That's against company policy.

Customer: I've only had the camera for a month.

Customer service representative: Unfortunately, when it leaves the store, it's yours unless you return it unopened in its original packaging.

Customer: You have got to be kidding.

Customer service representative: We do have other cameras available for purchase that are suitable for novice photographers.

Customer: I don't plan to return to your store again.

Customer service representative: Thank you for calling.

Part 3

Developing Professional Telephone Skills

Files You Will Need:

VC3-Y17.docx

VC3-Y18.docx

VC3-Y19.docx

VC3-Y20.docx

VC3-Y21.docx

VC3-Y22.docx

VC3-Y23.docx

VC3-TechWork.docx

VC3-IC1.docx

VC3-IC2.docx

Since its development in 1876 by Alexander Graham Bell, the telephone has become one of the most common home and business appliances. The word "telephone" comes from the Greek "tele," meaning at a distance, and "phone," meaning voice. According to the International Telecommunication Union, close to 5 billion people worldwide subscribe to telephone service. Of these, 4 billion are mobile or cellular customers. No matter where you live and work, you use a telephone in the workplace and should do so in a professional manner. In this unit, you learn the fundamentals of proper telephone etiquette. **case** You are a customer service representative in the Operations Department of Quest Specialty Travel and work with Nancy McDonald, the head of Customer Service. You spend most of your time on the phone, talking to Quest customers. Nancy is training new customer service representatives, and invites you to attend the sessions to review and help her train others in the essentials of professional telephone communication.

OBJECTIVES

16 Explore professional telephone communication

17 Place telephone calls

18 Receive telephone calls

19 Use voice mail

20 Leave professional messages

21 Take calls for other people

22 Screen, hold, and transfer calls

23 Develop cell phone etiquette

Exploring Professional Telephone Communication

In the workplace, you use the telephone to communicate with customers, colleagues, superiors, suppliers, and others—in short, everyone with whom you have a professional relationship. In some cases, such as when you are working with customers in other locations, the telephone is your primary channel for communication. The success of your business relationships therefore depends on your phone skills. Table 3-1 summarizes telephone communication do's and don'ts. ▶case▶ Before you meet with the new customer service representatives, Nancy McDonald suggests you review the fundamentals of professional telephone communication.

DETAILS

Observe the following guidelines as you use the telephone in professional settings:

QUICK TIP
Instead of interrupting someone with a phone call, consider sending an e-mail, instant, or voice-mail message.

- #### Use the telephone when it is appropriate

  Telephones are so convenient that you might reach for them out of habit. When you make a telephone call, you are taking up someone else's time in addition to your own. Before you call, ask yourself whether your call is necessary and appropriate. Would an e-mail message serve your purpose? Would it take less time to resolve the matter yourself or look up the information you need on your own? If you need to speak to someone you know is busy, send an e-mail message to schedule the phone call. Figure 3-1 shows when you should make a phone call or send an e-mail.

  Many people prefer the telephone as a communication channel because it is more personal than other channels except for face-to-face conversations. Take advantage of the intimacy and immediacy of the telephone to develop a relationship, respond to a matter quickly, or end a cycle of e-mail messages that raise more questions than they resolve.

- #### Identify yourself and your caller

  When the telephone rings, you seldom know who is calling or what to expect. Using **caller ID**, a feature that displays the phone number and sometimes the name of the caller, helps to identify your caller. When you answer the phone, immediately identify yourself by name and affiliation. Doing so prompts your callers to also identify themselves. If they don't, you can say, "May I ask who's calling?" If a phone call is your first contact with a customer, the way you answer the phone forms the customer's first impression of your business.

QUICK TIP
Provide frequent oral feedback so the speaker knows you are receiving and understanding the message.

- #### Remember that you lose the visual cues

  When you speak to someone face to face, much of the communication is nonverbal. When speaking on the telephone, keep in mind that you cannot convey these nonverbal cues. Take extra care to speak clearly, keep the volume of your voice moderate, and communicate your message carefully.

- #### Keep the conversation positive and cheerful

  Instead of responding to nonverbal cues, your listener picks up on the tone and inflections of your voice. When speaking to someone on the telephone, be as animated and enthusiastic as you would be if you were talking with them in person. See Figure 3-2. As they speak, some professionals watch themselves in a mirror, smile, or stand up when they make or answer a phone call. These actions help improve the tone of their voice.

- #### Use technology effectively

  Telephone service continues to develop with innovations in technology. Recent advances include sophisticated portable phones, satellite telephones, and Internet-based **telephony**, a technology for digitally transmitting voice across distances. Internet telephony uses the Internet instead of traditional phone lines and services to exchange voice communications. Consider how new developments might benefit you and your organization.

FIGURE 3-1: Choosing phone calls or e-mail messages

Make a phone call when you:

- Expect to exchange ideas or questions
- Make a personal contact
- Are contacting someone who has expressed a preference for the phone
- Want to take care of something routine, such as scheduling an appointment

Send an e-mail when you:

- Need information in writing
- Want to communicate with more than one person at the same time
- Want to schedule a phone call
- Plan to review your communications later
- Want to provide additional information as an attachment

FIGURE 3-2: Keep the conversation positive and cheerful

Ron Chapple studios/Photos.com

TABLE 3-1: Telephone communication do's and don'ts

guideline	do	don't
Choose the telephone	• Establish or enhance a relationship • Respond to a matter quickly • Avoid a time-consuming cycle of e-mail messages • Use this channel when others prefer it	• **Don't** call when you might interrupt someone • **Don't** ask someone the answer to a question you can find yourself • **Don't** set up routine meetings or introduce topics others need time to consider in a phone call
Identify yourself and the caller	• Use caller ID • Offer your name and affiliation when you answer the phone • Ask for the caller's name and affiliation	• **Don't** answer a business phone with a curt "Yes?" or even "Hello" • **Don't** chew gum, eat, or drink while you are on the phone
Use oral, not visual, cues	• Use a positive tone of voice • Animate your voice • Speak slowly and clearly • Moderate the volume of your voice • Smile as you speak	• **Don't** prop the phone between your shoulder and ear • **Don't** let your voice communicate fatigue, discouragement, or aloofness • **Don't** turn away from the phone while talking—doing so changes the volume on the receiver's end
Consider technology	• Take advantage of advances in telephone technology	• **Don't** assume your contact has the same technology that you do

Developing Professional Telephone Skills

Placing Telephone Calls

Placing a telephone call involves accessing a dial tone, entering the phone number of the person you want to contact, waiting while the recipient's telephone rings, and greeting the person who answers. Unless your recipients are expecting your call, consider that you might be interrupting them and disrupting their work. Respect other people's time when using the telephone by planning an agenda for the call, providing information when you introduce yourself, and conducting the call with efficiency. Table 3-2 lists the do's and don'ts for placing telephone calls. **case** You are preparing to call Carly Allbright, who represents SouthWest Insurance, a corporate customer of Quest Specialty Travel, to verify upcoming travel plans. Nancy McDonald discusses how you and the other customer service representatives should place telephone calls productively, as shown in Figure 3-3.

1. Organize your call before you make it

When you call someone for business, respect their time and act efficiently. You should know the purpose of your call and what you need to accomplish before dialing. Create a brief agenda for yourself. If you have several questions to ask or topics to discuss, write them down so you can stay focused.

2. Dial calls carefully

Because misdialing numbers creates unnecessary interruptions, take care to look at your keypad and double check the phone number as you enter it. If you accidentally misdial, politely apologize and explain that you have the wrong number. Simply hanging up is not only impolite, but can alarm the person answering the call.

3. Let the telephone ring

When placing calls, let the phone ring at least six times before hanging up. If the person you are calling is not next to their phone, they might be nearby. It is frustrating to run for a telephone call and hear a dial tone when you answer it.

4. Introduce yourself immediately

Unless you are calling a close friend who recognizes your voice, start every telephone call with a greeting followed by your name and the name of your organization. If your call is answered by a receptionist or someone else, ask for the person you want to speak to by name. For example, "Hello, this is Eric Jameson with Quest Specialty Travel. May I please speak with Carly Allbright?"

5. Follow up with the purpose of your call

Unsolicited business calls are not occasions to make light conversation as you would with friends. Follow your introduction with a short explanation of why you are calling. Ask if this is a convenient time for your recipient. If not, arrange a time to call back.

6. Conclude your calls promptly

If you initiate a telephone call, you are responsible for concluding it. Keep business calls short and listen carefully for signals suggesting that the other person wants to end the conversation. Thank people for taking the time to speak with you and for any help they have provided.

Practice making phone calls to customers by reorganizing a telephone conversation. Open the VC3-Y17.docx document and follow the steps in the worksheet. When you are finished, submit the document to your instructor as requested.

FIGURE 3-3: Placing a phone call to a Quest customer

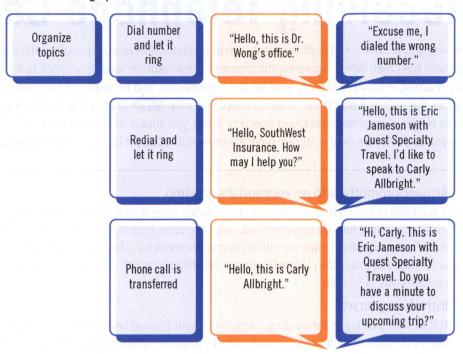

TABLE 3-2: Placing phone calls do's and don'ts

element	do	don't
Planning	• Create a brief agenda • List questions or topics you want to cover	• Don't lose focus or the thread of the conversation • Don't overlook the purpose or audience of your call • Don't call when it might be inconvenient for your recipient
Dialing	• Dial calls carefully • If you misdial, apologize and explain you reached the wrong number	• Don't dial while you are distracted with other matters • Don't hang up without apologizing if you dial the wrong number
Ringing	• Let the phone ring at least six times	• Don't hang up prematurely
Introducing yourself	• Start by announcing yourself by name and affiliation • Ask for the person you want to talk to by name	• Don't assume your recipient will recognize your voice • Don't fail to identify yourself if you are answering the phone for someone else
Explaining the purpose of your call	• Explain why you are calling • Ask if this is a convenient time for your recipient	• Don't assume that because someone picks up the phone that they are not otherwise occupied • Don't exchange pleasantries or chat during an unsolicited business call
Concluding	• If you placed the call, take responsibility for ending it • Listen for signals that the other person wants to end the conversation	• Don't interrupt or talk over the other person after you've fulfilled the purpose of your call • Don't forget to thank people for taking time to speak with you

Receiving Telephone Calls

The way you answer your telephone creates an immediate impression, especially if the call is your first contact with the caller. When answering the phone in the workplace, identify yourself to let callers know who they reached, establish a friendly tone for the conversation, and be responsive in general. Table 3-3 summarizes the do's and don'ts for receiving telephone calls. **case** During the course of your day as a customer service representative at Quest Specialty Travel, you answer dozens of phone calls. Nancy McDonald asks you to advise the new customer service representatives about how to receive telephone calls.

ESSENTIAL ELEMENTS

QUICK TIP
In the early days of the telephone, it was customary to greet your caller with the words "Ahoy-hoy."

1. **Answer promptly with an appropriate greeting**

   A good rule of thumb is to answer your phone within three rings if possible. If your caller hangs up prematurely, you might miss an important call. Greet the caller with "Hello," "Good morning," or "Good afternoon" as appropriate. Answering with short expressions such as "Yes?" "Uh-huh," or your last name sounds uninviting and makes the caller think you are otherwise occupied. Answer all of your calls as pleasantly and professionally as you can.

QUICK TIP
If you work in a small organization, omit the name of your department.

2. **Introduce yourself**

   Follow your greeting by introducing yourself with your first and last names and the name of your organization or department. If most of your calls come from people outside of your company, start with the name of the organization. For example, "Thank you for calling Quest Specialty Travel. This is Eric Jameson. How may I help you?" If most of your calls come from within the organization, use the name of your department: "This is Eric Jameson, Customer Service Department."

3. **Focus on your caller**

   Having a conversation with someone who is checking e-mail, reading the newspaper, or is otherwise distracted can be discouraging and unproductive. When you speak on the phone, focus your attention on the caller. Sit up in your chair and turn away from your work and computer when listening and talking. Doing this helps you sound respectful and responsive to your caller.

4. **Be prepared to talk**

   Do not chew gum, eat, or drink when talking on the telephone. Because the microphones in handsets and cell phones are sensitive, your caller will clearly hear the sounds that you are making. Remove any chewing gum or swallow food that you are eating before answering a telephone call. See Figure 3-4.

5. **Don't let the telephone interrupt you**

   If someone calls at an inconvenient time, let them know and offer to call back later. If you are especially busy or having an important meeting with someone, mute your ringer and let the call transfer to voice mail. Be sure to check these messages as soon as your schedule permits.

YOU TRY IT

Practice receiving phone calls by revising a telephone conversation. Open the VC3-Y18.docx document and follow the steps in the worksheet. When you are finished, submit the document to your instructor as requested.

FIGURE 3-4: **Be prepared to talk when you answer the phone**

Jupiterimages/Photos.com

TABLE 3-3: **Receiving phone calls do's and don'ts**

element	do	don't
Answering	Answer promptly, such as within three rings	Don't risk missing an important call
Greeting	Start with a standard greeting such as "Hello," "Good morning," or "Good afternoon"	Don't use expressions such as "Yes?", "Uh-huh," or your last name
Talking and listening	• Focus on the caller • Sit up in your chair and turn away from your desk and computer • If you receive a call at an inconvenient time, offer to call back later	• Don't check your e-mail or do something else that distracts you from the call • Don't answer the phone with anything in your mouth • Don't let a phone call interrupt you

Text message etiquette

According to a survey conducted by the Pew Research Center in September 2011, 83% of American adults own cell phones and 73% regularly send and receive text messages. The same survey found that most cell phone users send or receive 10 text messages daily, while they make or receive an average of 12 cell phone calls per day. Young adults "exchange an average of 109.5 messages on a normal day—that works out to more than 3,200 texts per month," which significantly increases text messaging as they take the habit into their professional lives. Because of this growing popularity, be aware of the following etiquette guidelines for sending and receiving text messages in the workplace:

* *Set your cell phone to vibrate*: To avoid interrupting colleagues, set your phone to vibrate when receiving text messages. If you are receiving only personal messages, it is better to turn off the phone completely.

* *Text at work only for work purposes*: Exchanging text messages can be an effective way to keep in touch with colleagues, but avoid doing so when you have other professional responsibilities.

* *Keep messages short*: Text messages are designed to be short and informal. Send longer messages via e-mail or cover a more formal topic in a phone call.

* *Avoid slangy shorthand*: Unless you're a teen writing personal messages, avoid using shorthand, which is far too informal in professional communication.

Sources: Smith, Aaron, "Americans and Text Messaging," Pew Internet, *www.pewinternet.org/Reports/2011/Cell-Phone-Texting-2011.aspx*, September 19, 2011; Reardon, Marguerite, "Americans Text More Than They Talk," CNET News, *http://news.cnet.com*, September 22, 2008.

Using Voice Mail

People expect someone to answer the telephone when they call a business during normal business hours. Some companies employ receptionists to answer calls for people in the organization. More often, businesses use answering machines and voice-mail systems to accept messages when employees are unavailable. **Voice-mail systems** connect telephones to computers that store messages. They play a prerecorded announcement to callers and allow them to record a short message. When setting up and using an answering machine or voice-mail system, be aware of the following guidelines to improve your caller's experience. Table 3-4 also lists the do's and don'ts for using voice mail. **case** Each Quest Specialty Travel employee has a voice-mail account so that callers can leave messages. Nancy McDonald reviews Quest policies for setting up and using the voice-mail system.

ESSENTIAL ELEMENTS

1. Record your own message

Record a personal greeting for your answering machine or voice-mail system. Avoid having someone else create a greeting for you or using the default recording. Because voice mail is an impersonal technology, using a voice other than your own makes leaving a message even less personal.

QUICK TIP
Write and print your message so you can practice a few times before recording it.

2. Keep your outgoing message short

Callers want to leave a message without having to listen to a lengthy announcement. When setting up your voice mail, record a concise, direct outgoing message. Start with your name so that callers know they have reached the right number. Next, outline the steps callers should follow, such as leaving their name, phone number to use when returning the call, best time to return the call, and a short message explaining the reason for the call. Figure 3-5 shows examples of outgoing messages.

3. Use a generic message for daily use

When you are in the office, but might be away from the phone from time to time, use a general message for your voice mail. Do not include a specific date in your announcement or other information that will quickly become obsolete. However, if your company requires messages to include dates or details, be sure to update your message each morning.

QUICK TIP
Make arrangements ahead of time if you refer callers to someone else.

4. Add detail if you will be away for more than 24 hours

Return calls within 24 hours under normal circumstances. In your outgoing message, let your callers know if you will be out of the office for more than a day. Start your outgoing message with a brief explanation and indicate when you expect to be back, as in, "I will be out of the office at a training session until June third." If possible, suggest that your callers contact someone else in your office for assistance.

QUICK TIP
If the other person is busy when you return calls, ask for a time when you should call back.

5. Check and return calls daily

Check your voice mail regularly—at least once each day. Keep track of new messages and return them promptly. If you cannot respond within one business day, send the caller an e-mail message or make a quick call to let them know that you will be delayed. See Figure 3-6.

6. Maintain your voice-mail inbox

Keep your inbox clean and organized. Reply to, forward, or delete messages immediately when you check them. Only save messages when you know you will need them in the future. Unnecessary messages make it difficult to browse and locate information that you need.

YOU TRY IT

Practice using voice mail by revising an outgoing voice mail message. Open the VC3-Y19.docx document and follow the steps in the worksheet. When you are finished, submit the document to your instructor as requested.

FIGURE 3-5: Examples of outgoing messages

Productive outgoing messages:

"Hello. You have reached the voice mail of Eric Jameson, customer service representative for Quest Specialty Travel."

"Please leave your name and the purpose of your call. Let me know when I should return your call and where I can reach you."

"Today is Monday and I'm out of the office at a company meeting. Please leave a message and I'll call you tomorrow."

Flawed outgoing messages:

"You've reached Eric. When you hear the beep, you know what to do."

"I can't get to the phone right now. Try again later."

"I'm either away from my desk or on the phone. Leave a message and I'll call you back when I can."

FIGURE 3-6: Check and return calls daily

Jose Maria Suria Ribera/Photos.com

TABLE 3-4: Receiving phone calls do's and don'ts

element	do	don't
Outgoing message	• Record a personal greeting • Keep the message concise and direct • Start with your name • Outline the steps callers should follow when leaving a message • Use a general message for daily purposes • Let callers know if you will be out of the office for more than a day • Suggest callers contact someone else in your office	• **Don't** use the standard greeting that ships with voice-mail systems • **Don't** let someone else record the outgoing message • **Don't** include unnecessary information or state the obvious, as in "I'm not available to take your call" • **Don't** mention specific dates for generic outgoing messages
Returning calls	• Check new messages regularly • Respond to messages promptly	• **Don't** wait for more than one business day to return a call • **Don't** lose track of when you receive messages

Leaving Professional Messages

When you place telephone calls, you often reach a voice-mail system instead of a person. The person you are calling might be out of the office, on another line, or out of range of their cellular carrier's service area. When this happens, you can leave a message. Making sure the message is professional increases the likelihood that your call will be listened to and returned in a timely manner. Table 3-5 summarizes the do's and don'ts for leaving messages. ▶ case ▶ When you call Quest customers and vendors, you often need to leave a message. Nancy McDonald asks you to describe messages that customers and vendors are most likely to return, as shown in Figure 3-7.

ESSENTIAL ELEMENTS

1. Speak slowly and clearly

Voice-mail systems convert your voice into a digital signal. Older answering machines record your message onto audio tape. Both approaches tend to suffer from low fidelity. Make it easy for people to hear and understand your message by speaking directly into your handset and enunciating your words.

2. Leave your name and telephone number

To increase the chances that your call will be returned, start and conclude your message by leaving your name and phone number. Don't assume the person you are calling knows how to get in touch with you. People are less likely to return a call if they have to search for your number.

3. Make it easy for the other person to write down your message

People usually review their voice-mail messages at one time and take notes as they do. Make it easy for the other person to write down the information that you want them to remember. In particular, state your name clearly and spell your last name. Articulate each digit of your phone number and repeat it. This gives the recipient time to correctly write down your details.

QUICK TIP
Cover a single idea or topic in your message.

4. Keep your messages short

Don't subject the people you call to a lengthy or complicated message. Many voice-mail systems stop recording after a certain amount of time, often without warning. Keep all of your messages short and direct to ensure that they are received and understood.

QUICK TIP
Mention specific times. "Call me at 2 p.m." is better than "Call me in a couple of hours."

5. Include the date and time that you called

Some voice-mail systems automatically include the time and date of your message, but not all do. It is courteous to briefly mention the date and time of your call and to suggest a good time to call you back.

6. Use basic courtesy

Use basic courtesy when leaving a voice-mail message. Don't indicate that you are frustrated or upset that no one was able to answer your call. Use expressions such as "please" and "thank you" when appropriate. Your recipient is more likely to return a polite call than an angry one.

YOU TRY IT

Practice leaving professional messages by revising a voice message. Open the VC3-Y20.docx document and follow the steps in the worksheet. When you are finished, submit the document to your instructor as requested.

FIGURE 3-7: Examples of messages

Effective message:	Flawed messages:
"This is Eric Jameson from Quest Specialty Travel at 619-555-1223. I have found a way to arrange the tour that you wanted. Please call me anytime before 5 p.m. Thank you."	"I'm calling to follow-up on our conversation. Call me when you can. This is Eric at Quest." "The reason for my call is that I'd like to see if you need further information about the matter we discussed..." "Eric at Quest 619-555-1223. Call me back."

TABLE 3-5: Leaving messages do's and don'ts

element	do	don't
Style	• Speak slowly and clearly • Give your recipient time to write down your name and phone number	• **Don't** rush your name and phone number • **Don't** force people to play back your message to hear essential details
Content	• Provide your name and phone number at the beginning and end of the message • Include the date and time that you called • Keep it short—15 to 40 seconds is long enough	• **Don't** assume your recipient has your phone number • **Don't** leave a long or complex message • **Don't** assume the system will record the date and time of your call • **Don't** reveal your frustration at having to leave a message

Instant interruptions

Phone calls, e-mail, text messages, and face-to-face conversations—all are contributing to an epidemic of interruptions. According to a study conducted in 2005, workers spend an average of only 11 minutes on a task before they are interrupted, and most interruptions (57%) are unrelated to their current task. For managers, the interruptions are *more* constant. They can expect an average of only three minutes of uninterrupted work on any one task before being interrupted by e-mail, instant message, phone call, co-worker, or other distraction. Tim McClintock of Global Knowledge Training offers the following time-management strategies for managing interruptions:

• *Reduce interruptions*: Screen your calls or close your office door when you need to focus on work. Don't let e-mail interrupt you—respond to messages when you are ready for them. Try checking e-mail only two or three times a day. If you do need to communicate with others, use the telephone instead of face-to-face meetings.

• *Take advantage of telephone technology*: Instead of answering all your phone calls, forward the calls to voice mail and then return them when you are free. Record an outgoing announcement that lets people know when to expect to hear from you. Let coworkers know when you are concentrating on a project and prefer not to be interrupted.

• *Anticipate interruptions*: If you find more than one colleague asking you for the same information, anticipate their needs and provide the information in an accessible place.

Sources: Mark, Gloria and Gonzalez, V., "No task left behind? Examining the nature of fragmented work," *http://portal.acm.org/citation.cfm?id=1055017*; McClintock, Tim, "Disrupt the Interrupters," *www.globalknowledge.com/training*, accessed March 18, 2009.

Objective 21 Part 3

Taking Calls for Other People

You might answer calls for someone else in your office as a routine part of your job or only as needed. In either case, remember that you are representing someone else and have an obligation to handle the call as professionally as you can. Table 3-6 lists the do's and don'ts for answering calls for other people. **case** → You often answer the phone for other customer service representatives and tour assistants when they are away from their desks. As you meet with the new customer service representatives, Nancy McDonald asks you to provide tips for taking calls for other people.

ESSENTIAL ELEMENTS

QUICK TIP
Not disclosing who you are can confuse callers and make them uncomfortable.

1. Let the caller know who you are

When answering for someone else, greet the caller by providing the name of the person you are answering for, and then identify yourself. For example, "Nancy McDonald's office, this is Eric Jameson, how may I help you?" lets the caller know they dialed the correct number and someone else is taking a message.

2. Avoid sharing details

Callers sometimes ask you for information about the person that they want to contact, such as "Do you know where they are?" and "When will they return?" Unless you are directed to share this information, avoid disclosing details, especially if they are confidential. The proper responses to such questions are that the person is not available, away from their desk, or out of the office.

QUICK TIP
Write messages on a preprinted form or pad so they are easy to read.

3. Take accurate messages

When taking messages for colleagues or superiors, they are relying on you to collect accurate information. Write down messages using a standard format instead of relying on memory. Ask for the correct spelling of each caller's name. Repeat the phone number and other details to ensure that you recorded them correctly. Organize the messages to make it easy for others to return the calls. Avoid overloading people with too many messages, and give messages to recipients as soon as they arrive. See Figure 3-8.

4. Keep the conversation brief and focused

If callers are contacting your colleague or superior to resolve a problem, they might try to involve you. However, it is not appropriate for you to step into a matter that concerns another person. In this case, avoid suggesting that the caller contact someone else in the organization. Politely indicate that you would be happy to take their name, telephone number, and a brief message, and let your colleague or superior continue to resolve the problem.

5. Avoid the "in a meeting" excuse

Avoid offering trite excuses such as, "He is in a meeting" or "She is in a conference." Instead of risking having callers doubt your sincerity, simply indicate that your colleague or superior is unavailable. See Figure 3-9.

YOU TRY IT

Practice taking calls for other people by revising a phone conversation. Open the VC3-Y21.docx document and follow the steps in the worksheet. When you are finished, submit the document to your instructor as requested.

FIGURE 3-8: Take accurate messages

Lai Leng Yiap/Photos.com

Comstock/Photos.com

FIGURE 3-9: Avoid the "in a meeting" excuse—just say your colleague is unavailable

Yanik Chauvin/Photos.com

TABLE 3-6: Taking calls do's and don'ts

element	do	don't
Greeting	Greet the caller by providing the name of the person you are answering for and your name	**Don't** pretend to be the person you are answering for or fail to identify yourself
Message	• Write down messages following a standard format • Verify the phone number and name • Provide messages to others as soon as they return	• **Don't** provide unauthorized details • **Don't** rely on memory • **Don't** step in and offer to try to resolve an ongoing problem • **Don't** offer trite excuses

Developing Professional Telephone Skills

Screening, Holding, and Transferring Calls

When working in an organization, you frequently handle calls that need to be routed to someone else. Even if a caller contacts you directly, another person in the company might be able to help them more than you can. In many instances, you can simply transfer the call to the intended person. In other cases, you might need to restrict transfers to certain callers and take messages from others. This process is called **screening** and is often used to avoid interrupting busy people. In both cases, you put the caller on hold, which is a way to suspend your connection without hanging up. Table 3-7 lists the do's and don'ts for handling phone calls. Figure 3-10 summarizes the process of answering, screening, transferring, and holding phone calls. ꞏcase➤ Nancy McDonald asks you to explain how to screen, transfer, and hold phone calls without frustrating people who contact Quest Specialty Travel by phone.

ESSENTIAL ELEMENTS

1. Put callers on hold when you leave the line

Use the hold feature when you need to move away from the phone. Do not set the phone or handset on your desk or muffle the microphone while you are talking to someone else. Telephone receivers amplify the noise, meaning the sound could be uncomfortable to the caller or the conversation audible anyway.

2. Ask before holding

If you abruptly put someone on hold, they might think you hung up on them. Instead, ask if they want to hold. Wait for their answer and respect their wishes. If they do not want to be put on hold, offer to take a message instead.

> **QUICK TIP**
> Some phone systems beep every 30 seconds or so while someone is on hold.

3. Check on callers frequently

When you place a caller on hold, check back with them every 30 seconds. Thank them for holding and provide them with your best estimate for how much longer they will have to wait. Each time you check the caller, offer them another opportunity to leave a message instead of staying on hold.

> **QUICK TIP**
> If your phone system supports it, announce the caller to your colleague before you complete the transfer.

4. Transfer calls carefully

If a caller needs to speak with someone else, ask if you should transfer the call. If they agree, ask for their telephone number in case they are disconnected in the process. Tell them who you are transferring them to. If a transfer is unsuccessful, call them back immediately and try to reconnect them to the person they requested. See Figure 3-11.

5. Screen calls courteously

If you are screening calls for a colleague or superior, be sure you do not create the impression that your coworker does not want to answer phone calls. When a caller asks for someone, indicate that he or she is unavailable, and then ask for the caller's name and nature of the call. Take a message if you are not transferring the call. If you do transfer the call, explain that you will try to reach the recipient.

YOU TRY IT

Practice screening calls by analyzing a phone conversation. Open the VC3-Y22.docx document and follow the steps in the worksheet. When you are finished, submit the document to your instructor as requested.

FIGURE 3-10: Handling phone calls

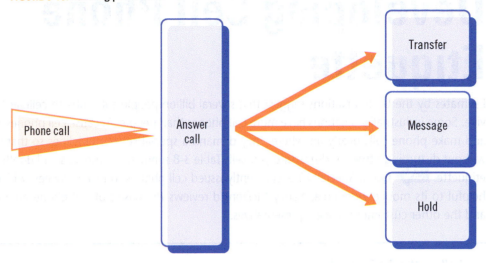

FIGURE 3-11: Transfer calls carefully

Ciaran Griffin/Photos.com

TABLE 3-7: Handling phone calls do's and don'ts

element	do	don't
Transfer	• Ask callers if they want to be transferred • Request their phone number in case they are disconnected	• **Don't** transfer a caller without warning • **Don't** transfer a caller unless you identify who might answer the phone by name
Screen	• Simply state your colleague or superior is unavailable • Ask for the caller's name and the nature of their call • Take a message if you are instructed not to transfer any calls	• **Don't** make it obvious that you are screening calls • **Don't** transfer screened calls unless your colleague or superior requests it
Hold	• Use the hold feature when you need to move away from the phone • Ask callers if they want to hold while you perform another task • Check frequently with callers on hold	• **Don't** set the telephone receiver on a hard surface or muffle the microphone • **Don't** put someone on hold abruptly • **Don't** put or leave someone on hold if they prefer to leave a message

Developing Professional Telephone Skills

Developing Cell Phone Etiquette

Estimates by the United Nations suggest that several billion people subscribe to cellular telephone service. Some industrialized nations have more cell phones than people. Because cell phones let you accept and make phone calls nearly anywhere, they demand a special set of guidelines so that you use them without disturbing others or distracting yourself. Table 3-8 summarizes the do's and don'ts of cell phone etiquette. **case** Quest Specialty Travel recently issued cell phones to its employees, which is especially helpful to its mobile workforce. Nancy McDonald reviews the basics of cell phone etiquette with you and the other customer service representatives.

1. **Follow the 10-foot rule**

   When speaking on your cell phone, maintain at least 10 feet between you and the nearest person. Even if you are speaking softly, you force others to listen to your conversation when you are closer than 10 feet, and you can become a nuisance.

2. **Be careful of "cell-yell"**

   Although microphones are designed to reduce background noise, some people raise their voice when speaking on a cell phone, which is disruptive to everyone around them. Speak softly when talking on a cell phone. If the other person can't hear you, they usually ask you to speak up.

3. **Maintain confidentiality in public**

   When using a cell phone in public, your conversation is open for all to see and hear. If you need to speak with someone about a private or business matter, maintain confidentiality by finding a private location before making the call. If someone calls you when you are in public, offer to call them back or ask them to hold while you move to another spot.

QUICK TIP

A subtle ring tone does not start with a loud or abrupt sound.

4. **Avoid loud and annoying ringtones**

   You can set up cell phones to play music, speech, sound effects, and other sounds as a call indicator. If you carry and use a cell phone in your professional role, use a basic, subtle ringtone. A gentle ring or simple tone alert is appropriate. Configure the phone to ring once and use a low volume.

QUICK TIP

If your phone rings by accident, turn it off. Don't compound the interruption by answering it.

5. **Turn off the phone**

   Turn off your cell phone before participating in a meeting, attending a class, or starting a job interview. See Figure 3-12. If possible, set the phone to vibrate or provide a silent indication that someone is calling. Cell phones must be completely turned off at funerals, weddings, religious services, and court proceedings. Also turn off the phone while driving. Talking on a cell phone while driving increases the risk of accidents, even when the driver uses a hands-free device with their cell phone. You are much safer if you pull over and stop your car before using a cell phone.

QUICK TIP

Don't wear a wireless earpiece when talking with someone face to face.

6. **Don't interrupt live conversations**

   When speaking with someone face to face, it is courteous to give them your full attention. Instead of allowing a ringing phone to interrupt a live conversation, let the phone transfer the caller to voice mail, and then return the call later.

Practice cell phone etiquette by analyzing a scenario involving a cell phone. Open the VC3-Y23.docx document and follow the steps in the worksheet. When you are finished, submit the document to your instructor as requested.

FIGURE 3-12: Don't let a cell phone interrupt a meeting

TABLE 3-8: Cell phone do's and don'ts

element	do	don't
Volume	• Stay at least 10 feet from others when you are talking on a cell phone in public • Use a standard ringtone that plays at a low volume • Turn off the phone during an interview, meeting, class, or conversation	• **Don't** feel you need to raise your voice when talking on a cell phone • **Don't** use an unprofessional or loud ringtone • **Don't** let your cell phone interrupt a professional gathering or face-to-face conversations
Conversations	• Maintain confidentiality • Set calls to transfer to voice mail when you are having a face-to-face conversation • Turn off the phone while driving • Pull over if you must make a call while driving	• **Don't** discuss private or business matters in public • **Don't** let cell phone calls interrupt a live conversation • **Don't** use the cell phone while driving

Technology @ Work: Voice over Internet Protocol

With **Voice over Internet Protocol (VoIP)** (also called broadband phone or Internet telephony), you can make phone calls using your high-speed Internet connection. Your voice travels across the Internet as data, similar to e-mail, allowing you to make long-distance phone calls for little or no cost. Because VoIP uses the Internet as its medium, it doesn't need to use the equipment provided by traditional phone companies, though those companies do offer VoIP options. To use VoIP, you contract with a VoIP service provider, such as Skype, Google Talk, or iChat for the Mac. Figure 3-13 shows the Skype Web page for businesses that want to use Skype VoIP services. Although VoIP has a few disadvantages (discussed below), it can cut phone expenses significantly, especially if you or your business makes a lot of long-distance calls. **case** Because Quest Specialty Travel makes many long-distance phone calls, it wants to see whether converting to VoIP would save money. Nancy McDonald asks you to investigate the basics of VoIP and to note its advantages and disadvantages.

1. **Decrease long-distance expenses**

   Most VoIP providers charge a monthly rate for their service, without additional charges for long-distance calls. In addition, popular and useful features such as call waiting, caller ID, hold, call forwarding, and multiple ring-to numbers are usually included with VoIP.

2. **Increase your mobility**

   Because VoIP uses the Internet, your phone number is not based on your physical location. You can make and answer phone calls using the same number no matter where you are. Many VoIP systems include telephony software you can use to send and receive calls with a headset connected to your computer. To do so, you can use a **softphone**, which is actually software, not hardware, which you install on a computer so you can make VoIP calls without a special telephone device. You can also use an Internet phone, a USB device that looks like a small phone with a speaker, microphone, and dialer.

3. **Store voice mail**

   For many voice-mail systems, you must retrieve messages from the phone system. Options for storing voice mail can be expensive. With VoIP, however, you can receive voice mail as e-mail messages and store them for later reference without incurring significant extra costs.

4. **Consider connection quality**

   One disadvantage of VoIP is that a low-quality Internet connection produces low-quality phone connections. Some calls suffer from an echo or a lag at the beginning of a conversation, while others are scratchy and uneven. Connection quality improves if you use special **IP phones**, which let you connect directly to a network without using a computer. See Figure 3-14.

5. **Protect against power failures**

   Although landlines and cell phones have independent power sources, a VoIP system is connected to the same power source as your computer. If you suffer a power failure that affects your computer network, you can lose your VoIP service.

Learn more about VoIP services by exploring the Skype Web site. Open the VC3-TechWork.docx document and follow the steps in the worksheet. When you are finished, submit the document to your instructor as requested.

FIGURE 3-13: Skype Web page for businesses

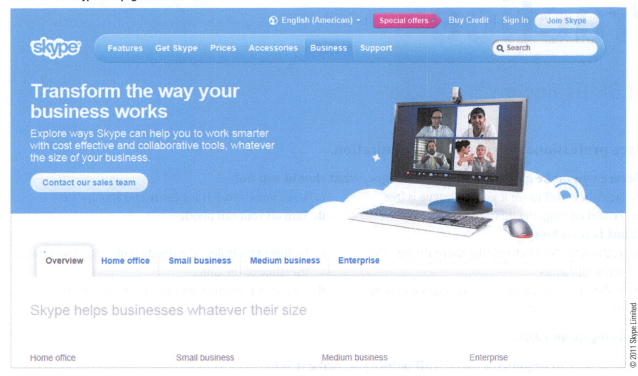

FIGURE 3-14: VoIP telephone

Practice

Soft Skills Review

Explore professional telephone communication.

1. **Before you make a phone call to a colleague, what should you do?**
   a. Send an e-mail to see if your colleague is free
   b. Record an outgoing message
   c. Make sure the call is necessary and appropriate
   d. Turn off your cell phone

2. **What is telephony?**
   a. Technology for electronically transmitting voice across distances
   b. System that lets callers leave messages and store them electronically
   c. Feature that displays the phone number and sometimes the name of the caller
   d. Process of restricting transfers to certain callers

Place telephone calls.

1. **A good way to organize a phone call before you make it is to:**
   a. learn how to use the hold feature
   b. write down a brief agenda
   c. practice speaking quickly
   d. store the phone numbers you need electronically

2. **When someone answers the phone, what should you do?**
   a. Assume they recognize your voice
   b. Announce your name and affiliation
   c. Start talking about the first item on your agenda
   d. Explain you don't have much time to talk

Receive telephone calls.

1. **A good rule of thumb is to answer your phone:**
   a. after the voice-mail system intercepts the call
   b. within six rings
   c. only if you know who is calling
   d. within three rings

2. **Which of the following should you *not* do when you receive a phone call?**
   a. Focus on the caller
   b. Turn away from your desk and computer
   c. Offer to call back later if the call comes at an inconvenient time
   d. Continue enjoying your snack

Use voice mail.

1. **What do voice-mail systems do?**
   a. Connect telephones to computers that store messages
   b. Send e-mail instead of voice messages
   c. Let you accept and make phone calls nearly anywhere
   d. Let you make VoIP calls without a special telephone device

2. **When you set up an outgoing message, you should:**
   a. use the standard greeting that ships with the system
   b. not reveal that you will be out of the office for a few days
   c. record a personal greeting
   d. assume the caller knows your name

Leave professional messages.

1. **What should you say if you leave a message for a customer and want them to call you back?**
   a. Entice them with the promise of a discount
   b. Suggest a good time to call you
   c. "Please call me" is sufficient
   d. Mention how many times you've called and left a message

2. **When you leave a message, you should:**
   a. assume your recipient has your phone number
   b. leave a long, complex message
   c. provide your name and phone number
   d. assume the system will record the date and time of your call

Take calls for other people.

1. **When answering the phone for a colleague, you should:**
   a. confide details about your colleague's absence
   b. get involved with an ongoing problem yourself
   c. say your colleague is in a meeting
   d. greet the caller by providing your colleague's name and your name

2. **Which of the following is *not* a guideline for taking accurate messages?**
   a. Write the message in a standard format
   b. Stick all the messages on your colleague's phone
   c. Ask for the correct spelling of each caller's name
   d. Give the messages to your colleague as soon as they arrive

Screen, hold, and transfer calls.

1. **What should you do before putting a caller on hold?**
   a. Ask if they can hold briefly
   b. Connect the caller to the voice-mail system
   c. Screen the call
   d. Let the phone ring six times

2. **Under what circumstances can you screen phone calls?**
   a. You need to step away from your desk
   b. A busy superior asks you to restrict transfers to certain callers
   c. A colleague is using a cell phone
   d. You think a colleague can better answer the caller's question

Develop cell phone etiquette.

1. **When you are in a public location and need to talk to a coworker on a cell phone about a business matter, what should you do?**
   a. Turn up the volume on the phone so you can hear your coworker
   b. Set up voice mail to record the call
   c. Find a private location before making the call
   d. Set the phone to vibrate

2. **Which of the following should you *not* do when using a cell phone?**
   a. Stay at least 10 feet from others when you are talking
   b. Raise your voice so your words are clear
   c. Use a standard ringtone that plays at a low volume on a cell phone in public
   d. Turn off the phone during an interview, meeting, class, or conversation

Technology @ work: Voice over Internet Protocol.

1. **What is Voice over Internet Protocol (VoIP)?**
   a. Technology for making phone calls using a high-speed
   b. Web site with voice-recognition software
   c. Wireless telephone deviceInternet connection
   d. Technology for recording outgoing phone messages

2. **Which of the following is *not* a benefit of using VoIP?**
   a. Maintain the same phone number
   b. Can store voice mail as e-mail messages
   c. Can make calls without a telephone
   d. Excellent connection quality

Critical Thinking Questions

1. **You are working on an important project at work that is due first thing tomorrow morning. However, you are having trouble concentrating on the project because you have been interrupted by a number of phone calls. What should you do?**

2. **One guideline in this unit is to turn off your cell phone when you are having a face-to-face conversation. How realistic is this guideline? Do you agree with it?**

3. **A recent study by Andrew Monk at the University of York found that bystanders observing public conversations conducted on cell phones and in person rated the cell phone conversations as more annoying. Predictably, they rated loud conversations as more unfavorable than quieter conversations. They also rated cell phone conversations more negatively than loud conversations. However, even when the volume of cell phone conversations was the same as in face-to-face conversations, study participants said using a cell phone made the conversation more annoying. Why do you think the study found these results?**

4. **Many businesses receive dozens of phone calls a day from telephone solicitors. Most solicitors offer legitimate products and services, but some do not. How do you think a small business should handle unsolicited sales calls? What about a larger business?**

5. **Your job involves making service calls to clients all around your city, so your company provides you with a high-end cell phone. Is it acceptable to use the same phone for personal calls?**

Independent Challenge 1

You work in the Customer Service Department at NorthStar, a four-season resort in eastern Maine. Kelly Mortensen, a supervisor at the resort, asks you to call Doug Wagner, who represents a software company in the northeast. Doug and the staff of the Research and Development Department at the software company have reserved the entire NorthStar resort for a few days of off-site business planning. Figure 3-15 shows the agenda for your call.

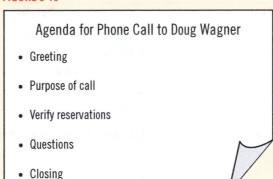

FIGURE 3-15

Agenda for Phone Call to Doug Wagner

- Greeting
- Purpose of call
- Verify reservations
- Questions
- Closing

a. Open the **VC3-IC1.docx** document and follow the steps in the worksheet.

b. Proofread the document carefully to fix any grammar or formatting errors.

c. Submit the document to your instructor as requested.

Independent Challenge 2

You work in the Bloomington Health Clinic, a family practice clinic in Bloomington, Indiana. As a patient service representative, you talk to patients and help solve their problems. Your supervisor has created the table shown in Figure 3-16 for handling standard types of phone calls from patients.

FIGURE 3-16

Step	Details
Identify caller	Find patient information in computer database: • Patient name • ID number • Phone number
Determine purpose	Ask about the purpose of the call
Caller wants to:	
Talk to someone else	Transfer
Ask question	• If you know the correct response, answer the question • If you don't know the answer, transfer the call
Schedule appointment	Schedule the appointment in the database
Resolve billing problem	• Call Billing Department • Provide patient ID • Transfer call

a. Open the **VC3-IC2.docx** document and follow the steps in the worksheet.

b. Proofread the document carefully to fix any grammar or formatting errors.

c. Submit the document to your instructor as requested.

Real Life Independent Challenge

This Real Life Independent Challenge requires an Internet connection.

You are preparing for a job search and want to enhance your skills so they are as appealing as possible to a potential employer. Most jobs involve interacting with customers, colleagues, or superiors on the phone. As with other professional skills, you can develop your telephone skills through observation, study, and practice.

a. Using your favorite search engine, search for tips on making and answering professional phone calls.

b. Search for particular telephone skills people in your chosen field of study need to develop.

c. When you receive phone calls from people representing companies, note how they handle the conversation.

d. In a word-processing document, list the telephone skills you want to adopt and those you want to avoid.

e. Proofread the document carefully to fix any grammar or formatting errors.

f. Submit the document to your instructor as requested.

g. Call your instructor and leave a voice-mail message that follows the guidelines in this lesson. The purpose of the call is to let your instructor know that you completed this Independent Challenge.

Team Challenge

You work for the Global Village, an import/export company specializing in products made from sustainable materials. Everyone at the company answers the phone and handles inquiries from customers and vendors, such as the following:

- Is Louisa Chen, head buyer, available? (Louisa Chen is often traveling.)
- Where do your products come from?
- Can I arrange a meeting with Ms. Chen?
- Can you resolve a shipping problem?

a. Meet as a team to assign the role of caller and receptionist.

b. Practice at least three telephone conversations based on the list of typical phone calls Global Village receives.

c. When you are not playing the role of caller or receptionist, take notes on telephone techniques you want to adopt.

d. Make sure each member of your team has a turn playing the role or caller, receptionist, and observer.

Be the Critic

Review the conversation shown in Figure 3-17 between a customer service representative at satellite radio company called In the Sky and a customer who wants to cancel his subscription. Analyze the conversation, noting its weaknesses, and send a list of the weaknesses to your instructor.

FIGURE 3-17

In the Sky: Hi, this is Ed at In the Sky. How can I help you today?

Mark: I want to cancel my subscription to In the Sky.

In the Sky: Okay. Is there a problem with our service?

Mark: No, but I don't use the service. I don't really listen to the radio much, so I don't need In the Sky anymore. I want to cancel.

In the Sky: But I can see from your customer account that you do use the service frequently. Last month, you recorded over 200 hours of service.

Mark: That can't be correct.

In the Sky: The record shows 212 hours of service.

Mark: Look, I want to cancel my account anyway.

In the Sky: I am happy to do that for you. But first explain why you are dissatisfied.

Mark: I am not dissatisfied and I don't want to explain anything. Just cancel the account.

In the Sky: Are you sure that's what you want?

Mark: I want to talk to your superior.

In the Sky: Sure. (puts Mark on hold.)

In the Sky: (5 minutes later) My superior is in a meeting. Can I help you?

Part 4

Improving Informal Communication

Files You Will Need:

VC4-Y25.docx

VC4-Y26.docx

VC4-Y27.docx

VC4-Y28.docx

VC4-Y29.docx

VC4-Y30.docx

VC4-Y31.docx

VC4-TechWork.docx

VC4-IC1.docx

VC4-IC2.docx

Oral communication in the workplace is often informal, and includes conversations and meetings. This type of communication is the basis of most professional relationships. Developing your informal communication skills means combining other oral communication skills to listen actively, respond with empathy, and speak persuasively. Most of the negotiation and problem-solving communication you do also involves informal oral communication. Enhancing these skills forms the foundation for your personal and career success. **case** You are a customer service representative in the Operations Department of Quest Specialty Travel and have been trained to communicate effectively with customers and solve their problems. Juan Ramirez, the personnel director at Quest, is organizing a series of meetings to discuss enhancing employee relations and improving internal communication at Quest, and asks you to help him organize and conduct the meetings. You plan to spend the next few weeks meeting with Juan, other customer service representatives, and the tour development staff to explore ways to improve teamwork among Quest employees and promote effective internal communication.

OBJECTIVES

24 Communicate informally

25 Listen actively

26 Speak persuasively

27 Negotiate effectively

28 Manage conflict

29 Participate in meetings

30 Deal with office politics

31 Make proper introductions

Alexander Raths

Communicating Informally

Because you communicate informally most of the time, it is easy to forget that any conversation on the job is still professional communication. Even if you are not making a formal presentation, you are *on stage* when you communicate with others in the workplace. Much of your informal communication is one on one, meaning that you are speaking with a single person as opposed to a group. This underscores the need to identify your purpose and audience. Take extra steps to make sure that your message is clear and understood. Listen carefully and be empathetic when expressing your ideas. Keep in mind that, like all business communication, the purpose of informal communication within an organization is to inform, persuade, and promote goodwill. See Figure 4-1. ▶case◀ Before you meet with Juan, you review the basics of informal communication within an organization.

DETAILS

Use informal communication opportunities to:

- ### Develop and strengthen personal relationships

  You form and enhance relationships through communication. Taking time to make a personal telephone call, briefly visiting colleagues at their desks when they are free, or discussing business over lunch help to foster goodwill among coworkers and decision makers. Business is built on friendships, connections, trust, and personal relations. Take advantage of opportunities to connect and communicate with other people in and outside of your organization.

  QUICK TIP
  To avoid sounding as if you are boasting, focus on objective, verifiable actions, and results.

- ### Promote yourself

  As you communicate with other people, you make yourself more visible and let others know what you are doing and accomplishing. In particular, let your managers and other decision makers know about your contributions to the organization. Decisions about raises, promotions, and other opportunities are often based on information that is gathered informally.

- ### Further your ideas and goals

  Decisions are seldom made in isolation. Much of what a successful professional does each day is to influence the decisions made by others. By talking about your projects, products, ideas, and goals, you inform others and keep them up to date with your activities. People tend to make decisions that favor the choices that are familiar to them. You can influence these choices through your communication.

When communicating informally:

QUICK TIP
Acting professionally also means maintaining an ethical standard of straightforward, objective communication.

- ### Act professionally

  Others form opinions of you based on what you say and do, and these opinions change frequently. When you interact with others, you are influencing their impression of you, whether you encounter them during the work day or afterwards. Consistently act and communicate with others in a professional manner. Be clear, objective, unbiased, and honest in your dealings, and people will want to do business with you.

- ### Emphasize the positive

  Businesses are often stressful environments where people overcome barriers to reach challenging goals. Don't add to stress by being negative, cynical, or critical in your communication. Professionals are optimistic and energetic when they speak. People feel better about themselves and their circumstances when you communicate with them in a positive way.

- ### Overcome obstacles

  Informal communication is often personal and directly connects you with other people. To maintain this direct connection, recognize the obstacles to effective communication so that you can minimize or overcome them. Table 4-1 lists typical obstacles to effective informal communication and offers suggestions for working around them.

FIGURE 4-1: Purpose of informal communication within an organization

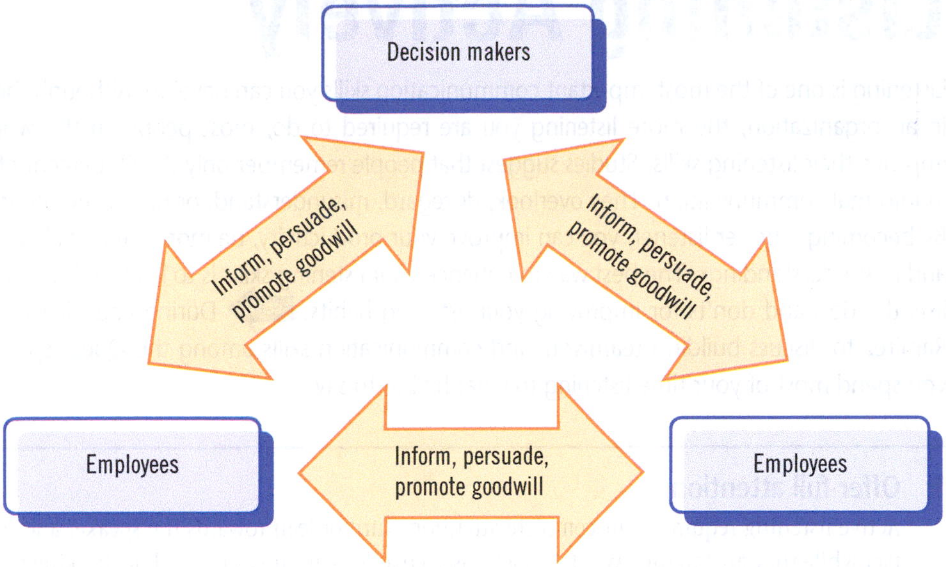

TABLE 4-1: Obstacles to informal communication

guideline	do	don't
Poor communication skills	Use plain English—short sentences, familiar words, and logical organization	Listen actively and request feedback frequently
Secondhand information	Cite your sources so others can verify your information	Seek information from original sources, such as direct conversation and official newsletters or Web sites
Distrust of employers or colleagues	Communicate more frequently and set an example by being candid	Provide positive feedback when receiving messages and honor requests for confidentiality
Competition	Give credit to others for ideas	Build teamwork skills to develop common goals
Bias	Use language that includes rather than excludes	Restate questions or comments using language that avoids bias

You heard it on the grapevine

Every organization has an informal communication network, or grapevine. The grapevine extends throughout the company, wherever two people get together and talk about their jobs, the organization, and other topics on their minds. One popular topic for the office grapevine is the economy, especially as it relates to job security. Juanita Ecker, president of Professional Image Management in Troy, New York, offers advice about grapevine etiquette. If you've heard through the grapevine that a colleague is getting laid off, Ecker recommends you wait for the colleague to introduce the topic. If they confide that they have lost their job and seem angry or indignant, express your support and discourage vengeful actions such as sending a former employer an accusatory e-mail message. Encourage your colleague to assess their strengths, not concentrate on mistakes or failures. According to Ecker, you should feel free to share job leads and provide books and articles, but don't offer client contacts or other types of references if you don't feel comfortable giving them.

Source: Lee, Louise, "Be Word Wary," *BusinessWeek*, April 3, 2009.

Listening Actively

Listening is one of the most important communication skills you can develop. Although the higher you rise in an organization, the more listening you are required to do, most people in the workplace need to improve their listening skills. Studies suggest that people remember only 25–50 percent of what they hear in informal communication. They overlook, disregard, misunderstand, or forget the other 50–75 percent. By becoming a better listener, you can improve your productivity, be more influential, and avoid conflicts and misunderstandings. The best way to enhance your listening skills is to learn to listen *actively*. Table 4-2 lists the do's and don'ts for improving your listening habits. **case** During your first meeting with Juan Ramirez to discuss building teamwork and communication skills among the Quest Specialty Travel staff, you spend most of your time listening to what he has to say.

ESSENTIAL ELEMENTS

1. Offer full attention

Active listening requires your complete attention. Turn or lean towards the speaker and maintain eye contact while they are talking. Avoid distractions such as looking at your e-mail or checking the time. Pay attention to the nonverbal signals that the other person is sending. Figure 4-2 outlines effective ways to listen to others within an organization.

> **QUICK TIP**
> Verbal cues such as "uh-huh" or "hmmm" also communicate interest and understanding.

2. Use nonverbal signals

Use your body language to signal your interest and attention to the other person. Let them know you are paying attention by occasionally nodding your head, smiling, or making appropriate facial expressions. Keep your arms unfolded and your hands unclenched. Providing nonverbal feedback doesn't necessarily mean that you agree with what the other person says, but does let them know you are actively listening.

> **QUICK TIP**
> Take notes to record details that you want to ask about or remember.

3. Give the other person feedback

Verify your understanding of the conversation by occasionally paraphrasing the other person's ideas and summarize what you think they are saying. Reflecting ideas back to the speaker helps both of you develop a common understanding and shows that you are interested.

4. Ask effective questions

Ask questions to clarify points or ideas that may be unclear. Even if you think that you understand the message, an occasional question shows the other person that you are carefully considering what they have to say. Use open-ended questions when you want to elicit more information. Use closed-ended (yes/no) questions when you need quick clarification on a point.

> **QUICK TIP**
> Communicate respectfully by treating others as you would like to be treated.

5. Keep an open mind instead of concentrating on an agenda

Focusing too much on your own questions, problems, and goals is a major distraction that interferes with your ability to actively listen and understand. Allow the speaker to finish a thought and try to listen with an open mind. Interruptions frustrate the other person and impede your ability to absorb and interpret their message. Save your answers for when they are finished talking, and give thoughtful responses.

YOU TRY IT

Practice listening actively by evaluating and responding to a conversation between a manager and a colleague. Open the VC4-Y25.docx document and follow the steps in the worksheet. When you are finished, submit the document to your instructor as requested.

FIGURE 4-2: Effective listening strategies

Colleague or superior says	Effective listening strategy
"I would like you to schedule regular team-building sessions for the staff."	Take notes and prepare follow-up questions
"I am not happy about all the extra time these meetings will require."	Let your colleague continue to talk
"I'm sorry to interrupt you, but I want to tell you something important before I forget."	Turn away from your computer and look your colleague in the eye

TABLE 4-2: Improving listening habits do's and don'ts

guidelines	do	don't
Pay attention	• Turn towards the speaker • Look directly at the speaker • Lean towards the speaker • Maintain eye contact with them while they are talking	• **Don't** be distracted by your e-mail, phone calls, or other external signals • **Don't** try to multitask and complete other jobs while listening
Use nonverbal cues	• Use your own body language to signal your interest and attention • Nod your head, smile, or make other appropriate facial expressions	• **Don't** fold your arms over your chest or clench your hands • **Don't** turn away from the speaker
Give feedback	• Paraphrase the speaker's ideas • Summarize what he or she says • Refer to notes to ask questions about details	• **Don't** be critical or argumentative in your feedback • **Don't** be afraid to disagree, but resist dismissing a message because you do
Ask questions	• Clarify points or vague ideas • Demonstrate you are carefully considering a speaker's message • Use open-ended questions to elicit more information • Use simple closed-ended questions for quick clarification	• **Don't** ask questions in a hostile manner • **Don't** be afraid to ask "dumb" or obvious questions
Be open-minded	• Allow the speaker to finish thoughts • Wait to respond until a speaker is finished talking	• **Don't** focus on your own questions, problems, and goals • **Don't** interrupt the speaker
Respond	• Provide appropriate responses • Be candid and honest • Maintain an attitude of respect • Treat others the way you would like to be treated	• **Don't** criticize the other person • **Don't** belittle their point of view

Improving Informal Communication

Speaking Persuasively

Persuasion is communication that guides people towards the adoption of an idea or action. To persuade others to take action or adopt an outlook relies on your ability to make appealing arguments instead of using pressure or coercion. Speaking persuasively and influencing others does not mean deceiving them into doing something they don't want to do. Instead, you often persuade others to convince them about the importance of their tasks, motivate them to perform, and request assistance and action. Figure 4-3 provides examples of persuasive messages. Table 4-3 lists the do's and don'ts for persuasion techniques. `case` Juan Ramirez has scheduled a voluntary meeting for anyone at Quest Specialty Travel who wants to discuss team-building goals. You want to persuade all of the customer service and tour development staffs to attend.

ESSENTIAL ELEMENTS

QUICK TIP
You can also increase a listener's receptiveness by using an enthusiastic, though soft, tone.

1. Choose an appropriate time

Persuasion is an emotional form of communication that others must be ready to receive. People who are upset, overwhelmed, or frustrated are not as open to persuasion. When speaking to a colleague or employer, make requests when you are both receptive and other pressing matters are not competing for attention.

2. Start with an offer

Salespeople frequently offer prospects refreshments, small gifts, or free samples early in the sales process. Offering something is a powerful way to start your communication. It sets a positive tone for the discussion and encourages the other person to reciprocate by offering you something in return. Simple offers can include compliments and information.

3. Emphasize the benefits

Effective persuasion emphasizes benefits to your listener. The desire for personal gain is a powerful motivator. Demonstrating how your idea, product, or service directly benefits the other person is more persuasive than explaining features. However, be careful not to exaggerate the benefits. People are sensitive to overly generous offers and often discount claims that sound too good to be true.

4. Plan for questions and contradictions

If you are trying to persuade others to adopt a new point of view, consider that they might be resistant to change. Acknowledge that they see the matter differently than you do. Expect them to ask questions and raise objections to the arguments that you make. Try to anticipate these concerns so you can respond to them confidently. You can often diffuse a problem by addressing it first.

QUICK TIP
Mirroring is sometimes called the chameleon effect.

5. Mirror the other person

Mirroring involves mimicking the body language and gestures of the person that you are trying to persuade. See Figure 4-4. When you act similarly to the other person, you demonstrate your empathy and sensitivity to them. Mirror their posture, hand gestures, and head movements. However, be subtle and wait several seconds before you mirror a behavior.

6. Do not lie or exaggerate

Honesty is not only a moral obligation, but a utilitarian one as well. Your ability to be persuasive is closely related to the reputation you have with coworkers and others. People will eventually uncover your dishonesty. When they do, you will have lost all credibility with them.

YOU TRY IT

Practice speaking persuasively by evaluating and responding to a persuasive conversation. Open the VC4-Y26.docx document and follow the steps in the worksheet. When you are finished, submit the document to your instructor as requested.

FIGURE 4-3: Examples of persuasive messages

Establish credibility:
"Other agencies have used these team-building techniques to improve company morale."

Overcome objections:
"I know you are busy this week, but the meeting could help you work more productively."

Make specific, reasonable request:
"Can you meet for one hour and bring one suggestion for improving company communications with you?"

Cite benefits:
"The meeting is designed to share ideas about making Quest a more satisfying place to work."

FIGURE 4-4: Mirror the other person

George Doyle/Photos.com

TABLE 4-3: Persuasion techniques do's and don'ts

guidelines	do	don't
Choose an appropriate time	• Make your argument when others are ready to receive it • Ask for what you want when other matters are not competing for attention	• **Don't** try to persuade people who are upset, overwhelmed, or frustrated • **Don't** introduce your argument when others are focused on something else
Start with an offer	• Offer a gift, sample, or idea • Provide something that can benefit the recipient	• **Don't** offer a gift that is out of proportion to your request • **Don't** decline a return offer
Emphasize benefits	• Provide evidence that shows how your idea can benefit your listener • Cite benefits that your listener cares about	• **Don't** make outrageous or unsupported claims • **Don't** cite benefits that are not important to your listener
Plan for questions	• Consider that listeners might be resistant to change • Anticipate objections • Prepare reasonable answers to likely questions	• **Don't** try to squelch resistance—listen objectively and overcome it • **Don't** ignore differing points of view
Mirror the listener	• Use the same body language and gestures as your listener • Demonstrate your empathy and sensitivity to your listener	**Don't** exaggerate the body language and gestures of your listener
Be honest	• Establish your credibility through honesty • Cite experiences and evidence that support your claims	• **Don't** make false claims • **Don't** pretend you are knowledgeable about a topic when you are not • **Don't** hide facts that might detract from your argument

Negotiating Effectively

Negotiation is a form of communication through which two or more people with different needs and goals try to identify a mutually acceptable solution to a problem. See Figure 4-5. Negotiation is common in business, government, legal, and personal relationships. Some people are uncomfortable negotiating with others because it often involves conflict. However, your career and personal success is influenced by how well you can negotiate with other people, so you should not avoid it. Table 4-4 lists the do's and don'ts for effective negotiation. **case** During the first team-building meeting with Quest customer service representatives and tour developers, Gail Owen, the developer of tours in Africa, wants to adopt a new procedure for handling customer complaints, and others in the Customer Service Department do not. You need to negotiate with participants to find a solution.

QUICK TIP
In many cultures, people are expected to negotiate to reach agreements on most prices, procedures, and policies.

1. **Claim the right to negotiate**

   In business, everything is negotiable. If you are not satisfied with the stated terms of an agreement or policy, don't be embarrassed to ask for something more favorable. Don't assume that a published price or offer is a take-it-or-leave-it proposition. Try to identify and work with someone who can authorize the different terms and options you want.

2. **Look for solutions acceptable to all sides**

   Some people approach a negotiation thinking that someone has to lose so that the other can win. However, you should look for a solution that meets the objectives of all participants. This is called "win-win" negotiation and should be your preferred approach. Thoughtfully considering your wants and needs in relation to others' wants and needs leads to a positive, satisfying outcome. Look for common ground and aim for an agreement that is fair to all. Figure 4-6 lists the steps for resolving conflicts in a negotiation.

3. **Establish your goals**

   Before you start to negotiate, identify what you hope to accomplish. Clearly list your objectives and keep these in mind as you negotiate. Establish what you will not agree to and terms that would not be acceptable. Consider the consequences of winning or losing the particular negotiation. Defining your goals in advance helps you to stay focused during the negotiation.

4. **Identify alternatives**

   Most negotiations involve compromises by participants. In many cases, the outcome can be more successful if you can identify alternatives that you would accept and minor objectives that you are willing to give up or exchange. For example, if a supplier is unwilling to lower a price, they might be willing to include something extra for the higher price. You might be able to request a bonus payment or extend vacation time in exchange for extra work to meet a deadline.

QUICK TIP
Doing your homework also helps you to know when to walk away from a bad deal.

5. **Do your homework**

   You negotiate more effectively if you do your homework first. Go online and research the issue. Find out competing prices, salaries, costs, or other information. Organize your findings and keep the information available in case you need it. Look for alternative solutions, sources, and options. Know what your next best option is in case you have to settle for it.

Practice negotiating effectively by negotiating a solution to a problem. Open the VC4-Y27.docx document and follow the steps in the worksheet. When you are finished, submit the document to your instructor as requested.

FIGURE 4-5: Negotiation works toward a mutually acceptable solution

Comstock Images/Photos.com

FIGURE 4-6: Steps for solving problems in negotiations

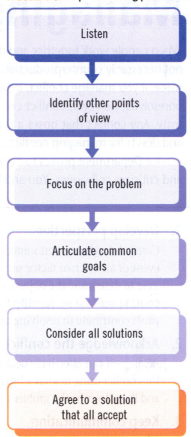

TABLE 4-4: Effective negotiation do's and don'ts

guidelines	do	don't
Claim the right	• Ask to negotiate an agreement • Identify and work with someone who can authorize different terms and options	• **Don't** be embarrassed to ask for a more favorable agreement • **Don't** assume that a published price or offer is the only possible offer
Look for solutions	• Find common ground • Introduce solutions that benefit most or all participants • Consider all points of view	• **Don't** approach the negotiation as if only one person can win • **Don't** discount a point of view • **Don't** eliminate solutions until you find agreement on one or more solutions
Establish goals	• Identify what you want to accomplish • List your desired outcomes • Establish acceptable and unacceptable outcomes	**Don't** fail to compromise on minor goals
Identify alternatives	• Find ways to exchange favors or services • Be open to alternatives	**Don't** overlook the needs and positions of others
Do research	Research the topic and find alternatives	**Don't** agree to something you don't fully understand

Improving Informal Communication

Managing Conflict

When people work together and depend on each other to get their jobs done, conflicts are inevitable, but not necessarily counterproductive. Disagreements and misunderstandings are a normal part of every workplace. If you manage conflict, it can help to clarify goals, enhance decision making, and build teams. If left unresolved, however, conflict can create disruptions in the workplace, reduce morale, and affect productivity. Any conflict that poses a threat to others should be addressed immediately. Table 4-5 lists the do's and don'ts for managing conflict. ▸case During the team-building meeting, one member of the Customer Service Department proves to be a distraction—he makes inappropriate comments, discounts suggestions, and criticizes colleagues. You and Juan need to manage the conflict he is creating.

To develop perspective, gather information, ask others for their interpretation and opinions, and consider how each person perceives the matter. Be prepared to see all points of view.

1. Develop perspective

Conflict develops when someone cannot achieve an objective—an external factor such as another person or event or an internal factor such as fear blocks the way to a goal. Before confronting a conflict directly, take time to determine the objectives of those in conflict, and the external obstacles or internal barriers that are creating frustration. Identify the concerns of each person and how the attitude and actions of all participants contribute to resolving or aggravating conflict, as shown in Figure 4-7.

2. Acknowledge the conflict

Before you can effectively deal with interpersonal conflict, you must understand the problem. Acknowledge the conflict using neutral, objective language. In a meeting or conversation, listen actively and empathetically and then describe the problem as you understand it. You might need to repeat these steps more than once.

Quickly changing your mind to avoid conflict and reach agreement rarely solves the underlying problem.

3. Keep communicating

Some people deal with conflict by withdrawing. However, avoiding a problem seldom solves it and can lead to a refusal to participate in general. Resolving conflict involves communicating and exchanging information and ideas. Choose the timing of your conflict-resolving conversations carefully, but don't try to avoid an uncomfortable discussion entirely.

4. Avoid manipulation and intimidation

Raising your voice, showing anger, or manipulating someone may stop a problem temporarily, but such techniques are often costly. In many cases, the problem resurfaces because it was not really resolved initially. If you do engage in negative behavior, apologize as soon as possible, and then demonstrate that you know how to be a constructive member of the organization.

Reacting calmly often diffuses someone else's anger.

5. Focus on the problem, not the individual

Most workplace conflict is caused by differences of opinion, expectations, and misunderstandings. Stay objective and keep the problem and personalities separate. The others who are involved will feel less threatened personally and be more willing to communicate and find a solution. Focusing on solving the problem can even improve relationships by showing that everyone is willing to come to an agreement. Figure 4-8 lists problem-solving techniques from mathematics and other fields, which also apply to organizational conflict.

Practice managing conflict by suggesting ways to handle group conflicts. Open the VC4-Y28.docx document and follow the steps in the worksheet. When you are finished, submit the document to your instructor as requested.

FIGURE 4-7: Reactions to conflict

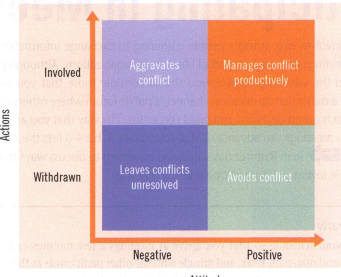

	Aggravates conflict	Manages conflict productively
	Leaves conflicts unresolved	Avoids conflict

Actions — Involved / Withdrawn
Attitude — Negative / Positive

FIGURE 4-8: Problem-solving techniques

Divide and conquer:
Break a large, complex problem into smaller, solvable problems (mathematics)

Brainstorming:
Encourage many solutions, withholding criticism and evaluation until later (social sciences)

Trial and error:
Apply possible solutions until you find the best one (physical sciences)

Analogy:
Discover how others have confronted and solved a similar problem (history)

TABLE 4-5: Managing conflict do's and don'ts

guidelines	do	don't
Develop perspective	• Take time to understand the problem or disagreement • Consider how the other person perceives the conflict • Be prepared to see all points of view	• **Don't** confront another person without considering their point of view • **Don't** belittle the suggestions, ideas, or contributions of others
Acknowledge the conflict	• Listen actively and empathetically • Acknowledge a difference in opinion or a misunderstanding using neutral, objective language	**Don't** assume you understand the problem
Keep communicating	• Continue to exchange information and ideas • Consider the timing of conflict-resolution conversations	• **Don't** withdraw from conflict • **Don't** try to avoid all conflicts
Control your emotions	• Apologize for unprofessional expressions of anger • Maintain your objectivity • Take a break as necessary	• **Don't** intimidate or manipulate others to get your way • **Don't** raise your voice or otherwise lose control of your anger
Focus on the problem	• Discuss the problem and how to solve it • Demonstrate that you understand other points of view	• **Don't** blame others for causing the problem • **Don't** reject ideas and suggestions from others

Improving Informal Communication

Participating in Meetings

A **meeting** involves two or more people gathering to exchange information, make decisions, and solve problems. Meetings are a regular part of life in most organizations. Although people sometimes joke about meetings and the time they require, you should consider those that you attend to be serious business. Meetings are a major communication channel, a public forum where others evaluate you, and offer opportunities to reach group decisions and build consensus. The way that you act, present your ideas, and work with others in meetings can advance or stall your career. Table 4-6 lists the do's and don'ts for participating in meetings. `case` Juan Ramirez has scheduled a meeting to discuss ways to improve the Quest customer experience. He invites you to participate in the meeting.

1. Arrive early

> **QUICK TIP**
> Most meetings are conducted by a leader, usually the person who organized the meeting and developed the agenda.

Manage your schedule so that you arrive at meetings a few minutes early. You can then organize your thoughts and materials, relax, and mingle with the other participants as they arrive. Don't disrupt a meeting by arriving late, rushing to your seat, and interrupting the proceedings. If a late arrival is unavoidable, let someone else know in advance so that the group does not wait for you to get started.

2. Come prepared to participate

Meetings are not a forum where you listen to other people speak. Rather, they are opportunities for everyone to actively participate in a discussion and exchange information. Review the agenda in advance and identify topics that affect you directly. The agenda should clarify the purpose and type of the meeting. Bring supporting materials with you in case you need to refer to them. See Figure 4-9. If you want to share printed information with others, make enough copies for everyone in attendance.

3. Contribute at least one message

> **QUICK TIP**
> Take responsibility for the quality of the meeting by offering feedback, commending others, and accepting assignments.

If you limit your participation in a meeting to answering other peoples' questions or listening quietly, you miss the opportunity to make a positive impression on the other attendees. Even if nothing on the agenda directly affects you, come to every meeting with a brief, prepared message that you can share. Offer a positive, concise idea at an appropriate time to make a memorable contribution.

4. Allow others to participate

Meetings are called so that everyone who attends has an opportunity to participate. Meetings become long and painful when one person tries to dominate the agenda. If you have an important point to make, do not hesitate to bring it up. However, be brief and direct so that others can contribute.

5. Show respect when others have the floor

> **QUICK TIP**
> Wait for a natural pause in the conversation or for the meeting leader to recognize you before you speak.

Show other participants the same respect you expect from them. Look at the person who is talking and actively listen to what they are saying. Take notes so you have a record of the discussion and decisions, but don't work on other projects, converse with others, or doodle during a meeting. Turn off your cell phone and avoid the temptation to check your e-mail or use other electronic gadgets.

Practice participating in meetings by suggesting ways to improve a meeting. Open the VC4-Y29.docx document and follow the steps in the worksheet. When you are finished, submit the document to your instructor as requested.

FIGURE 4-9: Come prepared to participate

Константин Чагин/Photos.com

TABLE 4-6: Participating in meetings do's and don'ts

guidelines	do	don't
Arrive early	• Show respect and demonstrate your organization skills by arriving early • Let the meeting leader know if you cannot avoid being late	• **Don't** disrupt the meeting if you arrive late • **Don't** expect the meeting leader to wait for you
Come prepared	• Be prepared for active, engaged participation • Review the agenda before you arrive • Identify topics of interest or importance to you • Bring supporting materials with you	• **Don't** sit back and listen to others • **Don't** ask the meeting leader or participants to cover material you should already know, such as the goal of the meeting
Contribute	• Prepare a comment, suggestion, idea, or other message to contribute during the meeting • Offer positive, concise ideas when appropriate	• **Don't** interrupt others to make your contribution • **Don't** restrict your contributions to answering questions
Conduct yourself professionally	• Maintain a professional demeanor • Pay attention • Provide positive comments • Speak with energy	• **Don't** use overly informal language • **Don't** make fun of the meeting or its agenda • **Don't** act bored with the meeting • **Don't** criticize others
Allow others to participate	• Keep your comments brief and to the point • React positively when others speak	• **Don't** withdraw if you are not interested in the agenda • **Don't** dominate the discussion
Show respect	• Make eye contact with the person who is talking • Demonstrate with your body language that you are listening actively • Take notes	• **Don't** work on other projects • **Don't** converse with others • **Don't** answer e-mail or your cell phone

Take charge of your meetings

If you are organizing and leading a meeting, you should focus on making sure the meeting is productive for everyone. Following are a few suggestions for conducting a professional meeting:

- *Start on time:* Start the meeting at the announced time, even if some participants are running late. Don't reinforce the idea that it's acceptable to be late.

- *Follow the agenda:* Distribute an agenda ahead of time, and then stick to it throughout the meeting. Keep yourself and others on track by politely steering them back to the topics listed on the agenda.

- *Encourage full participation:* As the meeting leader, your job is to fulfill the objectives of the meeting—solve a problem, communicate progress, or make a decision, for example. Focus on group dynamic—who is contributing and who is silent, for example—and encourage everyone to participate by asking questions and acknowledging contributions.

- *End on time:* Ending the meeting on time is just as important as starting on time. Be sure all participants know what they are expected to do after the meeting. Distribute notes and tasks as necessary to make sure the expectations are clear.

Verbal Communication

Dealing with Office Politics

The term **office politics** describes the interactions and relationships between people within an organization, usually focused on who is gaining or losing power and influence. Office politics is a regular part of the day-to-day culture of any business. When used to gain advantage at the expense of others or the well-being of the organization, office politics should be avoided. However, office politics can also be networking behavior that helps you fairly promote yourself and your career. Career experts believe that becoming involved with office politics helps you highlight your skills, draw attention to your accomplishments, and promote your success and upward progress. Table 4-7 lists office politics do's and don'ts. `case` You have been a customer service representative at Quest Specialty Travel for a year, and have recently accepted extra responsibilities and duties. You want to discuss a promotion with Nancy McDonald, your supervisor, but need to be aware of office politics to determine the best time to approach her.

ESSENTIAL ELEMENTS

1. ### Learn the company culture

   Every organization develops its own way of reaching its goals, conducting itself in the business world, and interacting with employees, customers, and others. Carefully observe and quickly adapt to your company's culture. Identify the core values and objectives of the organization. Determine how people communicate and how decisions are made. Learn about the reward structure, the types of behaviors that are valued, as well as the taboos you should avoid.

   > **QUICK TIP**
   > Volunteer to work on high-profile assignments and important tasks when they become available.

2. ### Support the company's goals and strategic initiatives

   Identify the projects, objectives, and initiatives that are most important to your organization, and contribute to them constructively. Update your skills so they match the company's needs. As your assignments mature, look for other opportunities to grow, develop, and contribute to the company.

3. ### Avoid taking sides

   People often form groups and factions within an organization, and these alliances can become powerful. However, changes in leadership can quickly shift the balance of power and result in new teams. Be careful about aligning yourself too closely with a group of people. If your plan is to work for a company for some time, a better strategy is to develop relationships with many people.

   > **QUICK TIP**
   > Remember that e-mail is not private and leaves a permanent record of what you said.

4. ### Communicate professionally at all times

   Organizations thrive on internal communication and information sharing. People often rely on networks of friends and colleagues to learn what is going on within the company, identify opportunities, and anticipate threats. However, gossip can be a destructive form of business communication. Be careful when chatting casually around the office, as in Figure 4-10. Assume that what you say will be public knowledge.

5. ### Treat people with respect

   People have long memories when they've been insulted, humiliated, or treated unfairly. Treat people professionally and with respect. Never embarrass someone in front of other people. Show basic courtesies whenever appropriate. People are more likely to cooperate with others who treat them well.

YOU TRY IT

Practice dealing with office politics by reacting to a scenario involving office politics. Open the **VC4-Y30.docx** document and follow the steps in the worksheet. When you are finished, submit the document to your instructor as requested.

FIGURE 4-10: Communicate professionally at all times

Comstock Images/Photos.com

TABLE 4-7: Office politics do's and don'ts

guidelines	do	don't
Learn the culture	• Observe and adapt to your company's culture • Identify the company's mission, values, and goals • Learn how decisions are made and the types of behaviors that are rewarded	• **Don't** assume your good work is being noticed • **Don't** ignore the company culture
Support goals	• Identify the goals and important projects of your organization • Develop the skills to meet your company's needs • Seek opportunities to improve your skills and contribute to the company	• **Don't** let your skills stay static • **Don't** avoid opportunities because they seem like extra work
Avoid taking sides	• Develop relationships with many people in your organization • Communicate with people at many levels of your organization	• **Don't** align yourself with one person or group • **Don't** exclude anyone from a professional relationship
Communicate professionally	• Network with colleagues and superiors • Maintain professional standards even in informal conversations	• **Don't** engage in destructive gossip • **Don't** assume that e-mail, voice mail, or other professional communication is private
Practice self-promotion	• Inform others about your accomplishments • Provide concrete evidence of your achievements • When you have the opportunity, let decision makers know about your contributions	**Don't** boast about your work if you can't substantiate your claims
Treat people with respect	Show basic common courtesy to everyone you work with	**Don't** insult, criticize, or humiliate anyone you work with

Making Proper Introductions

As you network throughout your career, you will meet many new people and introduce them to others. Making introductions correctly is a professional skill that can set you apart from others. When done correctly, introductions make people feel more comfortable in social and business settings. Proper introductions also encourage communication and foster good relationships. The rule in making introductions is to speak to the most important person first. Table 4-8 lists introduction do's and don'ts. **case** Greg Hamilton is a friend of your family and owns a popular resort in southern California named Oceanside Village. Greg wants to work with Quest Specialty Travel to offer special promotions. He asks you to introduce him to Ron Dawson, vice president of marketing, and Keisha Lane, vice president of operations.

ESSENTIAL ELEMENTS

QUICK TIP
Be sure to introduce people who don't know each other—it is uncomfortable for everyone if you don't.

1. Introduce others in social settings

In social situations, follow established forms of etiquette, even if they seem formal. For example, in a social setting, a man is introduced to a woman. A younger person should be introduced to an older person. Introduce everyone to a guest of honor regardless of their gender or age.

2. Introduce others in business settings

Make business introductions on the basis of rank in the organization, not gender and age. Present the person of lesser authority to the senior person. If appropriate, indicate the person's title or position in the company. For example, if you are training a new employee named Kristin Welford and run into Keisha Lane, say, "Keisha Lane, I'd like to present Kristin Welford. Kristin is new in the Customer Service Department. Kristin, this is our vice president of operations, Keisha Lane."

QUICK TIP
Pronounce your name clearly when introducing yourself.

3. Introduce clients and customers

Clients and customers are the basis of a business' profitability, and should be considered the most important person when making introductions. Use the client's name first when making introductions. Follow this guideline even if you are introducing a customer to the president of your company. For example, introduce Greg Hamilton to Ron Dawson by saying, "Greg Hamilton, I'd like you to meet Ron Dawson. Ron, this is Greg Hamilton, the owner of Oceanside Village."

4. Introduce one person to a group

Occasionally, you need to introduce a single individual to a group of people in social and business settings. In such situations, address the single individual first and then present the group members to them. Give the names of the group members in the order in which each person is standing or sitting.

5. Introduce yourself

Sometimes you need to introduce yourself to other people. This is appropriate in social and business settings when you meet someone for the first time. When introducing yourself, extend your right hand, greet the person, and give your name. Even at a meeting with others you know, take time to introduce yourself to people you do not know. See Figure 4-11.

YOU TRY IT

Practice making proper introductions by reacting to a scenario involving introductions. Open the VC4-Y31.docx document and follow the steps in the worksheet. When you are finished, submit the document to your instructor as requested.

FIGURE 4-11: Introduce yourself at a meeting

Jacob Wackerhausen/Photos.com

TABLE 4-8: Introduction do's and don'ts

guidelines	do	don't
Social	• Follow established forms of etiquette • Introduce a man to a woman, and a younger person to an older person • Introduce everyone to a guest of honor	**Don't** ignore established practices because they seem formal
Business	• Make introductions based on rank in the organization • Present the person of lesser authority to the senior person • Include titles if appropriate	**Don't** consider gender and age in business introductions
Clients and customers	• Introduce the customer to people in your organization • Use the customer's or client's name first	**Don't** forget that your business depends on your customers
One person and a group	• Introduce a single person to a group of people • Name people in the group in the order in which they are standing or sitting	**Don't** skip the introductions if it seems tedious to make them
Self-introduction	• Introduce yourself when you meet someone for the first time • Extend your hand for a handshake	**Don't** fail to pronounce your name clearly
Acknowledge introduction	Respond with a greeting and offer to shake hands	**Don't** act as if you are not interested in meeting someone
Forms of address	Address colleagues according to your relationship with them	**Don't** use informal forms of address with superiors or when the relationship status is unclear

Technology @ Work: Microblogging Tools

A **microblog** is an online service that lets you exchange very short messages with others by combining the features of blogging, text messaging, and social networking. Currently, the most popular microblog is Twitter, which has attracted millions of users since it launched in 2006. Twitter fans like the immediacy of the service, and use it to ask and answer questions, learn from others, share resources, and react to events throughout the day. Critics say it is another electronic distraction in a world full of them. In business, you might use Twitter to communicate with others in your organization or search for Twitter users who fit the profile of your typical customer or client. If they are interested in your company or product, they can establish conversations with you on Twitter. You can exchange ideas with them and provide links to your company's Web site, articles, Webcasts, and press releases. You can also search Twitter content for information about your company to respond to complaints and other comments. **case** Juan Ramirez is interested in using Twitter to communicate with tour developers and others at Quest when they are on the road. He asks you how to find out how to use Twitter.

1. **Create a Twitter account**

   Visit the Twitter Web site at *www.twitter.com* and sign in to create a free account. See Figure 4-12. Use your full name as your user name, if possible, so you are clearly identified to others.

2. **Add a personal photo**

   Click your name, click Settings, and then click Profile to add your photo to your account. Your communications display your photo along with your text.

3. **Provide a short, biographical description**

   On your Profile page, enter a brief biographical description. This identifies you to others and helps you find people who share your interests.

4. **Post messages**

   Tweets are text messages of up to 140 characters. Use your tweets to exchange professional information with others, answer questions, and develop business relationships.

5. **Follow others**

   One way to develop business relationships is to search for people who have posted messages in areas of your interest. For example, if you are developing a tour to New Zealand, search for *New Zealand travel*. The search results lists people and organizations involved in travel to New Zealand. If they seem especially interesting, you can click their photographs and then click the Follow button to invite them to follow you or to receive your tweets. See Figure 4-13.

Practice working with Twitter or another microblogging tool. Open the VC4-TechWork.docx document and follow the steps in the worksheet. When you are finished, submit the document to your instructor as requested.

FIGURE 4-12: Creating a Twitter account

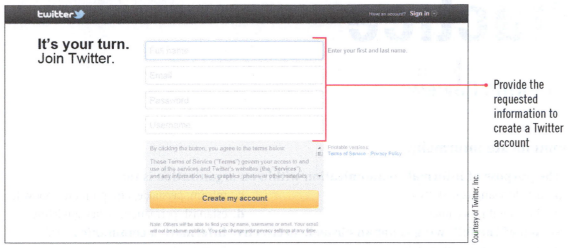

Provide the requested information to create a Twitter account

Courtesy of Twitter, Inc.

FIGURE 4-13: Finding people and businesses on Twitter

Follow button

Courtesy of Twitter, Inc. (TK)

Verbal Communication

Practice

Soft Skills Review

Communicate informally.

1. **The purpose of informal communication within an organization is to:**
   - **a.** develop language skills
   - **b.** document procedures
   - **c.** inform, persuade, and promote goodwill
   - **d.** establish permanent policy guidelines
2. **Which of the following is *not* an obstacle to effective information communication?**
   - **a.** Poor communication skills
   - **b.** Staff meetings
   - **c.** Competition
   - **d.** Bias

Listen actively.

1. **How can you practice active listening?**
   - **a.** Turn toward the speaker and make eye contact
   - **b.** Check the time to stay on schedule
   - **c.** Disregard nonverbal signals to focus on the words
   - **d.** Stay on top of your projects by responding to e-mail
2. **What types of questions should you ask to show you are listening to a speaker's message?**
   - **a.** Those that clarify points or vague ideas
   - **b.** Open-ended questions
   - **c.** Closed-ended questions
   - **d.** All of the above

Speak persuasively.

1. **What does speaking persuasively involve?**
   - **a.** Deceiving others into taking action
   - **b.** Guiding others to adopt an idea
   - **c.** Pressuring someone to make a donation
   - **d.** Disregarding the flaws in your idea
2. **Why should you mirror someone when you are speaking persuasively?**
   - **a.** To keep them from getting complacent
   - **b.** To solve problems
   - **c.** To demonstrate your empathy with them
   - **d.** To show them how they look

Negotiate effectively.

1. **What is negotiation?**
   - **a.** Communicating to identify a mutually acceptable solution to a problem
   - **b.** Mimicking the body language and gestures of another person
   - **c.** An obstacle to effective interpersonal communication
   - **d.** Communicating to plan a meeting
2. **What should you do as you look for solutions in a negotiation?**
   - **a.** Approach the discussion as if only one person can win
   - **b.** Discount competing points of view
   - **c.** Eliminate the most difficult solutions
   - **d.** Look for common ground

Manage conflict.

1. Conflict in the workplace:

a. should be avoided at all costs

b. is a normal part of every business

c. is a signal the business is in trouble

d. creates customer relation problems

2. What should you do to manage conflict effectively?

a. Keep communicating

b. Focus on the problem, not the person

c. Avoid manipulation and intimidation

d. All of the above

Participate in meetings.

1. Which of the following is *not* a goal of a meeting?

a. Exchange information

b. Fill free time

c. Make decisions

d. Solve problems

2. Before attending a meeting, you should:

a. find a comfortable chair so you can listen to other people speak

b. review the agenda

c. plan to arrive shortly after the stated start time

d. organize work to do during the meeting

Deal with office politics.

1. What can you do to participate in office politics effectively?

a. Learn the company culture

b. Eavesdrop on gossip around the water cooler

c. Align yourself with successful employees

d. Assume that if you keep quiet, others will notice your work

2. Which of the following is *not* a way to promote yourself within a company?

a. Develop skills to meet your company's needs

b. Seek opportunities to improve your skills

c. Identify the goals of your organization

d. Look for ways to downplay the success of others

Make proper introductions.

1. Why should you learn to make proper introductions?

a. They promote office politics

b. They provide an outline for a meeting

c. They are a dying art

d. They make people feel more comfortable

2. When you arrive at a meeting with a new member of the staff, you should:

a. introduce yourself first

b. introduce the women first

c. introduce the new member of the staff first

d. introduce the meeting leader first

Technology @ work: Microblogging tools.

1. How is a microblog different from a blog?

a. You exchange very short messages

b. You are discouraged from expressing an opinion

c. You post photos, not text

d. You assume a virtual identity

2. You can post messages on Twitter to:

a. provide a detailed analysis of other microbloggers

b. download music and audio files

c. exchange professional information with others

d. eventually create a Web site

Critical Thinking Questions

1. You overhead the following comment during your first week at a new job: "Book learning and technical know-how are not enough to advance a career." Do you agree or disagree?

2. Many guidelines for communication include tailoring your message for your audience. Do you think this is a guideline you will follow as much as possible? Why or why not?

3. Suppose you are helping to organize a meeting to solve a problem of retail theft where you work. What types of strategies will you use to encourage productive discussion?

4. Companies and trade organizations develop ethical guidelines or codes of conducts for their field. For example, the Association for Computing Machinery (ACM) has a code of conduct for computing professionals (see www.acm.org/about/code-of-ethics). Should all professions develop similar codes? How effective do you think they are?

5. You have been meeting with colleagues to find a way to complete an important project at your company. After several meetings over lunch, you and the members of your team reach a consensus during the third meeting and find a solution acceptable to everyone. Later that day, you overhear one of the team members taking credit for the solution. What do you do?

Independent Challenge 1

You work in the Customer Service Department at NorthStar, a four-season resort in eastern Maine. Kelly Mortensen, a supervisor at the resort, is planning to host a meeting with investors in the resort and raise additional operating funds. She has prepared the agenda shown in Figure 4-14.

a. Open the **VC4-IC1.docx** document and follow the steps in the worksheet.

b. Proofread the document carefully to fix any grammar or formatting errors.

c. Submit the document to your instructor as requested.

FIGURE 4-14

Agenda

NorthStar Resort
Investor Meeting

1.   Brainstorming session

    Questions and answer session
    Announcements

2.   Department reports

3.   Introductions

4.   Approval of minutes of staff meeting

5.   Financial report

6.   Business goals

    Winter conferences
    Web site update
    Customer newsletter/blog

7.   Summary

Independent Challenge 2

You work in the Bloomington Health Clinic, a family practice clinic in Bloomington, Indiana. As a patient service representative, you talk to patients and help solve their problems. Your supervisor has enrolled you in a training session in Orlando, Florida, and encourages you to extend the trip over the weekend. One of your colleagues in the Patient Services Department feels this is unfair and demands to go to the training session in your place because she is less experienced and needs the training more than you do.

a. Open the **VC4-IC2.docx** document and follow the steps in the worksheet.

b. Proofread the document carefully to fix any grammar or formatting errors.

c. Submit the document to your instructor as requested.

Real Life Independent Challenge

This Independent Challenge requires an Internet connection.

You are preparing for a job search and want to enhance your skills so they are as appealing as possible to a potential employer. Many career coaches identify the ability to plan and conduct effective meetings as an essential job skill, one that often leads to promotions. As with other professional skills, you can develop your meeting skills through observation, study, and practice.

a. Using your favorite search engine, search for tips on planning and conducting meetings.

b. If possible, attend meetings and observe how others conduct them.

c. In a word-processing document, list at least five meeting skills you want to adopt. Also list at least five meeting practices you want to avoid.

d. Proofread the document carefully to fix any grammar or formatting errors.

e. Submit the document to your instructor as requested.

Team Challenge

You work for Global Village, an import/export company specializing in products made from sustainable materials. On the phone and in person, you often deal with people who do not speak English as their first language. As a team, meet to discuss the following topics:

- What special challenges do nonnative speakers have in a business environment?
- What special challenges do members of an organization have when dealing with nonnative speakers?
- How can you improve communication?
- What guidelines can you follow to improve intercultural communication?

a. Reach a consensus on the answers to these questions.

b. On your own, summarize the guidelines you identified.

Be the Critic

Review the conversation shown in Figure 4-15 between two colleagues at an accounting firm—Jen and Adam. Analyze the conversation, noting its weaknesses, and send a list of the weaknesses to your instructor.

FIGURE 4-15

Jen (having a loud phone conversation): The place was fabulous. We can't wait to go there again!

Adam: Jen, excuse me. I'm trying to get some work done over here.

Jen (hanging up): Excuse me?

Adam: I'm glad you had a fun weekend, but it's tax season, and I need to concentrate.

Jen: What, were you eavesdropping on my conversation?

Adam: Do you know how loud your voice is?

Jen: Do you know how rude you are?

Adam: Fine, I won't say a thing. I'll request some soundproof earphones from our manager.

Jen: You do that. I'll request a transfer to a different part of the department.

Making Formal Presentations

Files You Will Need:

VC5-Y33.docx

VC5-Y34.docx

VC5-Y35.docx

VC5-Y36.docx

VC5-Y37.docx

VC5-Y38.docx

VC5-Y39.docx

VC5-TechWork.docx

VC5-IC1.docx

VC5-IC2.docx

Speaking is a soft skill you use informally to accomplish everyday tasks. More formally, a verbal presentation is a popular and efficient way to help people understand your idea, project, or proposal. Public speaking puts you on the stage and on display for those in attendance. To be an effective public speaker, you need to learn how to use your voice, body language, and visual aids to capture and hold peoples' interest. This is one of the most valuable professional skills that you can develop, and it will serve you throughout your career. **case** You are a customer service representative in the Operations Department of Quest Specialty Travel and work with Nancy McDonald, the head of Customer Service. Nancy and other managers at Quest realize that everyone in the company needs to provide top-notch customer service. Nancy asks you to prepare a presentation on customer service and give it during an upcoming company meeting.

OBJECTIVES

32 Plan effective presentations

33 Develop presentation content

34 Rehearse a presentation

35 Deliver a presentation

36 Build rapport

37 Manage anxiety

38 Use appropriate visuals

39 Manage questions and answers

Objective

32

Part 5

Planning Effective Presentations

Mark Twain once observed that, "It usually takes me more than three weeks to prepare a good impromptu speech." You also need to carefully plan and prepare your oral presentation when asked to speak. Time invested in planning will pay off as you develop, rehearse, and finally deliver your speech. Regardless of your topic, audience, or forum, the following guidelines will help you craft an effective presentation. Table 5-1 outlines when to give an oral presentation and when to use other forms of communication. **case** Before you start working on your customer service presentation, you decide to review the basics of making presentations.

DETAILS

Keep the following guidelines in mind when you are asked to speak publicly:

QUICK TIP

Your presentation should focus on only a few basic ideas.

• ### Refine your message

As you start planning your presentation, write your main idea on a piece of paper the size of a business card. If you can't fit your message in that space, it is too complicated. A good presentation includes a simple main theme that can be supported by several points or ideas. Know the purpose of the presentation so you can refine the message.

• ### Anticipate your audience

As you begin your planning, carefully consider who your audience will be. Who are they? Why are they listening to you? How familiar are they with your topic? What will their interest level be? What should they take away from your presentation? Answer these questions before you begin, and keep the answers in mind as you develop and deliver your speech. Figure 5-1 lists questions to ask to analyze your audience.

QUICK TIP

Asking what your manager wants is a good way to define the purpose of the presentation.

• ### Ask what your manager wants

Your manager or meeting planner asked you to speak for a particular reason. Meet with them to identify what they want you to accomplish. Clarify the expectations of your speech or presentation, including details such as the number and type of people in the audience, how long you should speak, and the scope of your content. If appropriate, consider the other topics on the agenda to be sure your material fits with the rest of the program.

• ### Budget enough planning time

Inexperienced speakers tend to underestimate the amount the amount of time it takes to develop and rehearse a formal presentation. Professional speakers often budget 10 or more hours of preparation for one hour of actual delivery. A formal presentation to a large audience requires more time than a casual speech to a small group. However, you should start planning well in advance for any presentation you are giving.

• ### Anticipate the extras

As you develop your speech, plan for the materials you will need to support your presentation. Don't assume that a projector, laptop, or microphone will automatically be set up. Find out who is responsible for these and notify them of your needs in advance. Check on your support materials before the meeting starts and have a backup plan in case something falls through. Enlist the help of a colleague to distribute handouts, dim the lights, and assist you as needed.

FIGURE 5-1: Analyzing an audience

Profile
- Do you know most members of the audience?
- What facts do you know, such as their age group and job positions?

Interest
- How much interest does your audience have in the topic?
- How can your information benefit your audience?

Attitude
- What is your audience's attitude toward you?
- What is their attitude toward your subject?

Content
- How much does your audience know about your topic?
- What do you expect your audience to do with the information you provide?

TABLE 5-1: Appropriate uses for presentations

scenario	give presentation	write report	use other
You are teaching colleagues how to perform a basic task	•		
You are summarizing the results of a customer survey	•		
Many people need to hear about company news at the same time	•		
Your manager asks you to propose an employee fitness program	•		
You want to persuade customers to try a new product or service	•		
You want to recommend a training session you attended	•		
You are explaining a complicated procedure people will refer to often		•	
You are proposing a new way to handle customer phone calls		•	
You are assisting on a detailed plan to expand your department		•	
You want to quickly congratulate a coworker about a promotion			Phone call, visit, or personal note
You want to resolve a problem regarding your employment contract			Face-to-face meeting
Your department needs to discuss a sensitive personnel issue			Private meeting

Presentation design tips

Following are the top five design tips from presentation professionals:

- *Keep it simple:* Leave plenty of white space on your slides. The less graphical clutter you have on a slide, the more powerful your visual message becomes.
- *Follow the six by six rule:* Include no more than six lines of text on a slide, and no more than six words in each line. Slides should support your speech, not make you unnecessary.
- *Limit special effects:* You don't need to use animations on every slide, especially if they're slow. In the same way, you don't need to use transition effects between all slides. Using the same effect creates visual consistency.
- *Use high-quality graphics:* Avoid cartoonish or common clip art, and take advantage of high-quality graphics, especially photographs, available for purchase online.
- *Use color effectively:* In particular, make sure you display light text on a dark background or dark text on a light background.

Developing Presentation Content

Unlike the president of the United States and executives from major companies, who rely on professional speech writers to develop their presentations and press releases, you are your own speech writer and develop your own material. Fortunately, effective presentations follow a simple three-step formula you can adapt to your situation. The following guidelines will help as you develop your ideas and refine them into a professional presentation. ▸case After meeting with Nancy McDonald to clarify the purpose and audience of your oral presentation on customer service, you are ready to develop the content.

1. Include the three major parts of a speech

Most well-developed presentations include three main sections: the opening, body, and conclusion. In the opening, start by catching your audience's attention and offer them a preview of your topic. In the body section, you should deliver your main message along with supporting ideas and information. The conclusion summarizes your main ideas. See Figure 5-2.

QUICK TIP

During the introduction, display a visual such as a slide that outlines your presentation.

2. Show your organization to the audience

Give your audience a simple map to follow so they can anticipate the format of your presentation. Doing so helps them understand what you are going to say next. Use a simple introduction such as, "I will begin by defining customer service in general. Next, I'll explain the current approach at Quest Specialty Travel. I'll conclude with ideas for developing our program." Outlining the organization lets people know what your topic is and how you will cover it.

QUICK TIP

Use an odd number of main points, such as "three steps to sales success."

3. Create a storyboard of your presentation

Most speakers change their presentation several times as they develop it. A **storyboard** is a planning tool that makes it easy to visualize your speech and edit it. Write each of your ideas on an index card and arrange them in order so you can quickly see your topics. To change the presentation, you simply reorder the index cards.

4. Write for the ear

Most of your preparation will involve visual material. You will be reading and writing as you develop your speech. However, your audience will be listening to your presentation and absorbing most of your message as oral communication. Nearly everyone processes information they hear more slowly than images they see. Keep your language simple, direct, and easy to understand.

5. Include attention-getters

It is difficult for an audience to stay attentive, especially if you are giving a presentation in a darkened room. Their attention will drift in and out as you are speaking. Help maintain their focus by including attention-getting devices every three to four minutes in your presentation. Attention getters are different from your normal speaking and catch the attention of your audience, such as pictures, props, video clips, stories, and short activities for the audience to participate in. See Figure 5-3.

Practice developing presentation content by reorganizing a presentation. Open the VC5-Y33.docx document and follow the steps in the worksheet. When you are finished, submit the document to your instructor as requested.

FIGURE 5-2: Three parts of a presentation

Introduction
- Catch the attention of the audience
  Ask question
  Tell humorous story
  Provide a startling fact
- Preview your topics
  Identify three main points
  Show slide with outline

Body
- Main message
  Organize logically, such as pro/con, chronological, or problem/solution
- Supporting ideas
  Cite evidence as in a written report
  Use comparisons, statistics, and anecdotes

Conclusion
- Summary
  Recap the main ideas and themes
- Exit line
  Use language such as "In conclusion"
  Repeat memorable line

FIGURE 5-3: Attention-getting devices

Show pictures or photos

Play a video or video clip

Tell a story

Lead an activity

Verbal Communication

Rehearsing a Presentation

An interesting paradox about public speaking is that it takes lots of preparation to sound spontaneous. Effective speakers know that the more they practice their material, the more naturally they deliver the speech. When you master the content of the speech, you will feel more comfortable adjusting your rate of speech, adding pauses, and including suitable gestures and movements. Table 5-2 outlines the do's and don'ts for rehearsing a presentation. `case`▸ Now that you've set the content of presentation on customer service, you are ready to practice giving the presentation. Nancy McDonald offers to listen to a rehearsal.

**ESSENTIAL
ELEMENTS**

QUICK TIP
Practice in front of a mirror so you can see yourself and make adjustments as you rehearse.

1. Practice as though you are delivering your speech

Reading your material quietly at your desk does have some value, but it can't take the place of active rehearsal. If you will be on your feet when you deliver your speech, stand up when you practice. Rehearse out loud as often as you can. Find a place where you can move, gesture, and experiment. See Figure 5-4.

2. Record yourself (audio)

Record yourself delivering your speech on a portable device, such as a smartphone. Listen to this recording as often as you can. Review your delivery while driving, working out, or shopping to become more familiar with the material and help you memorize key parts of your presentation.

QUICK TIP
When your presentation looks and sounds good on camera, you are ready for the audience.

3. Record yourself (video)

Record a video of yourself practicing your speech. Use a simple camcorder or a **digital video recorder**, which is a camera that records video in a format you can play on your computer. Recording yourself with a camera is a powerful rehearsal technique because it provides candid feedback. The camera records everything you do, good or bad, so you can review your facial expressions, gestures, and nervous habits.

4. Ask someone to critique you

It is often hard to see the problems in your own presentation. Enlisting someone to critique your performance helps you polish these rough spots. Have a trusted friend, colleague, or family member watch you rehearse your entire presentation. Try to deliver your speech as you would in front of an audience. Ask them to be honest and constructive with their feedback. In particular, have them rate your opening and conclusion because these are the most important parts of the presentation.

5. Use visualization

Visualization is the technique of forming a mental image or vision of yourself performing a task and can be a useful tool as you prepare a presentation. Imagine yourself delivering your presentation. Close your eyes and develop a mental picture of being introduced, speaking confidently, and your audience applauding. Psychologists have found that your brain interprets the visualizations as real events, which will help you to feel more comfortable when you make your speech.

QUICK TIP
Most audiences grow restless after 20 minutes, so use that as the maximum length for the presentation.

6. Rehearse a dry run

If you can access the room where you will make your speech, rehearse there before anyone else arrives. Go through your presentation and make sure everything is working properly. Walk around the speaking area, and sit in the seats. Seeing yourself from your audience's perspective helps you decide where to stand, move, and how loudly you need to speak. See Figure 5-5.

YOU TRY IT

Review how to rehearse a presentation by describing how to prepare for an oral presentation. Open the VC5-Y34.docx document and follow the steps in the worksheet. When you are finished, submit the document to your instructor as requested.

FIGURE 5-4: Practice as though you are delivering your speech

Sandra Gligorijevic/Photos.com

FIGURE 5-5: Steps in a successful rehearsal

Know your subject thoroughly

↓

Practice the entire presentation

↓

Time yourself

↓

Check the room

↓

Relax

↓

Greet members of audience as they arrive

TABLE 5-2: Rehearsing do's and don'ts

guidelines	do	don't
Rehearse	• Stand up when you practice if you will give your presentation on your feet • Practice your speech out loud • Try out various movements and gestures • Visualize your performance • Rehearse in the same place you will give the presentation • Walk around the presentation room and view the speaker's area as the audience sees it	• **Don't** only read your material at your desk • **Don't** arrive in the room where you will present without allowing time for a rehearsal
Record	• Make an audio recording of your speech and play it to learn your delivery and content • Record a video of yourself practicing your speech	• **Don't** assume you know how you sound to others • **Don't** fail to learn from the recordings—you can improve your pronunciation and performance
Critique	• Ask a colleague, manager, or friend to watch and critique your presentation • Deliver the speech as you would in front of an audience • Ask others to rate your opening and conclusion	**Don't** take critical suggestions personally—improve your presentation based on the comments of others

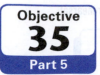

Delivering a Presentation

The moment of truth arrives when you finally stand to make your presentation. This is where you reap the benefits of the time and effort that you put into careful planning and rehearsal. When you start your delivery, remember that your speech is partly a performance. The way you speak, move, and interact with your audience influences how people react to what you say. Keep the basic principles of speech delivery in mind as you rehearse and deliver your presentation. Table 5-3 lists the do's and don'ts of delivering your presentation. case ▶ The Quest Specialty Travel staff is assembled for a day of off-site meetings and presentations. You are giving your presentation on customer service in a few minutes, and are reviewing the fundamentals of delivering a presentation professionally.

**ESSENTIAL
ELEMENTS**

1. Gesture appropriately

Your hands can help you communicate an idea if you use them appropriately. Most people use their hands in everyday conversation. Gestures help reinforce what you are saying and make you more visible when speaking to a large audience. When gesturing, let what you say trigger the action. For example, shrug your shoulders when you are asking a question, or extend your fingers when counting to add a visual dimension to your words. Refrain from exaggerating gestures, which can seem insincere in a presentation.

2. Use the power of pauses

Pausing occasionally during your presentation can dramatically increase the impact of your words People pay more attention when the incoming information suddenly stops. You can use either short or long pauses. See Figure 5-6.

QUICK TIP
Bring two sets of speaker's notes. Keep one set in your pocket just in case.

3. Speak naturally—don't read your speech

Inexperienced speakers often write out their speeches and recite them to the audience. Others copy their speech to PowerPoint slides and read the bullet points from the screen. Both approaches are painful for the audience and reflect poorly on the presenter. Instead, write notes on index cards that you can glance at occasionally. If you've properly rehearsed, a simple outline should be enough to guide you.

QUICK TIP
It is proper etiquette to use a microphone if one is available.

4. Use a sound system or public address system

If people can't hear you, they won't understand your message. Using a microphone and sound system or the public address system, if one is available, makes it easier for everyone to understand what you are saying. Don't assume that your voice is loud enough for all to hear. People seated in the back of the room or who have hearing difficulties appreciate the added volume.

QUICK TIP
Don't rely on the housekeeping staff to test everything before the meeting begins.

5. Walk as you talk

Move around as you speak, but not so much that you are distracting. Your movements and body language can evoke interest, reinforce the emotions of your stories and punctuate a change of pace or topic. If a lectern is available, use it to hold your laptop, water bottle, and speaker's notes. Don't stand behind the lectern unless it has the only available microphone or the formality of your presentation requires it.

6. Have a backup plan

In case of power failures, equipment malfunctions, and other unforeseen problems, have a backup plan. Bring visuals and support materials that don't require the use of an electrical outlet. A second laptop, spare bulb for the projector, and a copy of your presentation on a USB drive can help you recover quickly if the unexpected happens.

YOU TRY IT

Practice delivering a presentation by analyzing one and then describing how to change it. Open the VC5-Y35.docx document and follow the steps in the worksheet. When you are finished, submit the document to your instructor as requested.

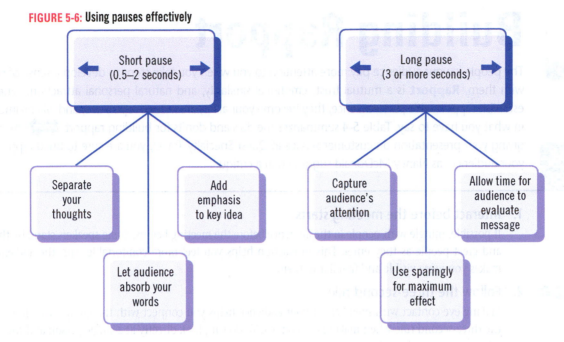

FIGURE 5-6: Using pauses effectively

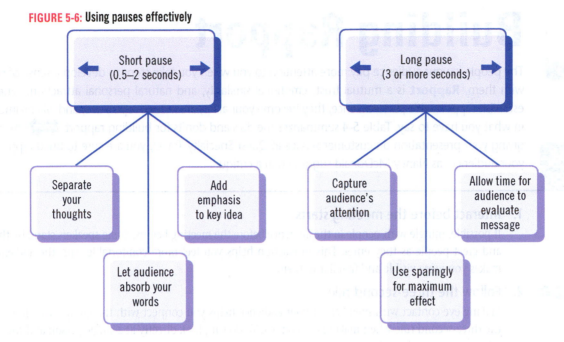

FIGURE 5-6: Using pauses effectively

Short pause (0.5–2 seconds)
- Separate your thoughts
- Let audience absorb your words
- Add emphasis to key idea

Long pause (3 or more seconds)
- Capture audience's attention
- Use sparingly for maximum effect
- Allow time for audience to evaluate message

Verbal Communication

TABLE 5-3: Presentation delivery do's and don'ts

guidelines	do	don't
Gestures	• Let gestures reinforce what you are saying • Make yourself more visible when speaking to a large audience • Let what you say trigger the action • Move around the room	• **Don't** stand still and deliver your presentation • **Don't** force gestures that don't seem natural • **Don't** hide behind a lectern
Speech	• Pause occasionally to keep the audience attentive • Speak conversationally • Use a microphone and sound system if possible	• **Don't** drone on without pausing • **Don't** read your speech or notes • **Don't** read the bullet points in an electronic presentation • **Don't** assume everyone can hear you
Support materials	• Bring printed handouts and other materials in case of a power failure or equipment problems • Pack extra equipment you might need	• **Don't** forget to develop a backup plan • **Don't** apologize if equipment fails—keep the presentation going

Delivering presentations to three types of audiences

Each member of your audience has a dominant learning style—visual, auditory (hearing), or kinesthetic (touching or moving). Your presentation will be more compelling and dynamic if it addresses each type of learning style. In a *BusinessWeek* column, Carmine Gallo outlines the three types of audiences. He says that about 40 percent of people are visual learners, so be sure to include plenty of meaningful images such as photos, graphics, and charts. He relates an incident involving a California woman who persuaded her neighbors and city council to review a proposed timber harvesting campaign in a nearby forest. The secret to her success? A presentation with images from Google Earth, the satellite mapping service, that showed the impact the timber harvesting would have on the area. "The visual was so striking," Gallo explains, "that former Vice President Al Gore came out against the project after he saw it." Gallo also identifies about 20 to 30 percent of audiences as auditory learners, those who benefit the most from powerful words and stories. Literary devices such as metaphors, analogies, and concrete examples also work well with auditory learners. The third type of audience, Gallo says, "learns by doing, moving, and touching. In short, they're 'hands-on.' They get bored listening for long periods of time." To engage these kinesthetic types of learners, include demonstrations and other activities that involve the audience and get them out of their seats.

Source: Gallo, Carmine, "Presentations with Something for Everyone," *BusinessWeek*, December 5, 2006.

Building Rapport

The people in your audience pay more attention to you when you take steps to develop a sense of rapport with them. **Rapport** is a mutual trust, emotional similarity, and natural personal attraction. When you establish rapport with your audience, they become your allies, are more cooperative, and will be interested in what you have to say. Table 5-4 summarizes the do's and don'ts for building rapport. case As you are giving your presentation on customer service at Quest Specialty Travel, you are sure to build rapport with your audience, as Nancy McDonald suggested in a critique.

1. **Interact before the meeting starts**

   If possible, mingle with people in the audience before the meeting begins. Some speakers stand by the door and greet people as they enter. This interaction helps you feel more comfortable with the audience and makes you more visible and familiar to them.

   QUICK TIP
   Looking people in the eye makes you more credible and believable.

2. **Follow the three-second rule**

   Making eye contact with members of your audience helps you connect with the group as a whole. Follow the three-second rule when making eye contact. To do this, look directly at a single person and then maintain your gaze and speak for at least three seconds. When you pause to take a breath, look at someone else and begin the process again. Move your attention to different sides of the room so everyone feels involved. Avoid shifting your gaze while you are speaking.

3. **Minimize the distance**

   When speaking, position yourself as close to the audience as you can. Distance between you is a barrier to interaction. Avoid using a riser or podium unless it is necessary for you to be seen. If you are speaking from a podium or stage, connect with the audience by frequently moving to face different people. See Figure 5-7.

4. **Illuminate your face**

   People in the audience want to see you as you speak. In particular, they want to see your face and will not develop a connection with you until they can see your eyes and sense your emotion. If you are not showing slides, make certain that all the lights are on. If you do need to dim the lights, try to stand away from the screen in a part of the room that is still lit. Some speakers arrange for a soft light to be set up that will illuminate their face in an otherwise dark room. Avoid talking to your audience from a dark part of the room. See Figure 5-8.

   QUICK TIP
   Don't say anything that would offend or embarrass anyone in the audience.

5. **Make your examples personal**

   When appropriate, use stories and examples involving you or someone else in the audience. If you are the subject of the example, be careful not to paint yourself as the hero or expert. Explaining how you struggled with a problem or poking fun at yourself in a self-deprecating way endears you to your audience. Sharing a story about someone in the group that others recognize and respect can be very powerful. Be sure to ask the person's permission before including them in your speech.

YOU TRY IT

Practice building rapport by suggesting ways to improve rapport between a speaker and audience. Open the VC5-Y36.docx document and follow the steps in the worksheet. When you are finished, submit the document to your instructor as requested.

FIGURE 5-7: Minimize the distance between you and your audience

FIGURE 5-8: Illuminate your face

TABLE 5-4: Building rapport do's and don'ts

guidelines	do	don't
Interactions	• Greet attendees as they arrive • Make yourself visible to your audience so they become familiar with you • Stay as close to the audience as possible	• **Don't** hide behind a lectern or offstage before the presentation • **Don't** reveal your stage fright • **Don't** use a riser or podium if you have the choice
Eye contact	• Follow the three-second rule and maintain eye contact with one person for three seconds • Move your attention around the room • Turn slightly to make direct eye contact	• **Don't** shift your gaze while you are speaking; wait until you pause • **Don't** focus on one or only a few people
Lighting	• Illuminate your face so your audience can see you • If you must darken the room, kept part of it lit and stay in the light	**Don't** dim the lights unless you are presenting slides
Examples	• Use yourself and members of your audience in your examples • Explain how you solved a problem • Use self-deprecating humor	• **Don't** digress from your outline • **Don't** provide anecdotes or examples where you are the hero or expert • **Don't** tell a story about someone in the audience without their permission

Managing Anxiety

Performance anxiety, often referred to as **stage fright**, is a psychological reaction to a person's fear of public embarrassment. People often feel stage fright when they are required to perform in front of an audience, especially if they are inexperienced public speakers. **Glossophobia** is the fear of public speaking and is the most common of all human phobias. Most stage fright actually arises while you are anticipating your performance. When you start to speak, much of the fear quickly goes away. Table 5-5 outlines the do's and don'ts for managing your anxiety about public speaking. **case** Your presentation is going so well, it's hard to imagine that you had stage fright before it started. The day before the presentation, you and Nancy McDonald reviewed the basics of avoiding stage fright.

QUICK TIP
Prepare for how you will look to your audience, too, by dressing appropriately for your speech.

1. Be well prepared

Performance anxiety is caused by our fear of making a mistake in front of other people. When you are unfamiliar with your material, you are more likely to be nervous. Careful preparation and practice helps to reduce your anxiety, though it cannot completely eliminate it. Keep in mind that nearly all public speakers experience anxiety, even the best ones. See Figure 5-9.

2. Loosen up before you speak

When you start to feel anxious, your body tightens in response. This can impair your ability to move, gesture, and speak. Exercise is an antidote to stress. Arrive early and take a brisk walk for at least five minutes. Stretch your legs, move your arms, and rotate your head and neck. Some speakers chew gum or yawn repeatedly to loosen their mouth and throat beforehand. See Figure 5-10.

3. Remember to breathe

Many speakers forget to breathe when they start to speak. Take some deep breaths before you begin to oxygenate your body. Pause occasionally during your speech and take a deep breath or two. Smile, if appropriate, during these breaks. Not only will this add effect to the presentation, but it will calm your nerves and improve your energy level.

QUICK TIP
Be careful not to drink too much water before you start.

4. Keep some water handy

A dry mouth is a common symptom of stage fright. It also makes it difficult to speak, which can lead to more anxiety. Keep a glass of water or water bottle handy when you present. Drink a small amount before you begin. Pause to take a sip if necessary. Avoid drinking milk, caffeinated drinks, or alcohol. Tepid water or herbal teas are the preferred drinks of professional speakers.

5. Don't apologize

Never tell your audience you are nervous or apologize when you make a minor mistake. No one but you knows the script and few people will notice if you don't call attention to yourself. Try to act confident instead. Eventually, you will feel more confident as you get into the body of your presentation.

QUICK TIP
Making eye contact with people that are smiling will help you feel better about your audience.

6. Remember the audience wants you to succeed

Performance anxiety is due in large part to a subconscious fear of how your audience will react to your presentation. Keep in mind that the people you are speaking to want you to succeed. They hope that you will do a good job and will overlook small mistakes that you make.

Practice managing anxiety by suggesting how a presenter can overcome anxiety during a presentation. Open the VC5-Y37.docx document and follow the steps in the worksheet. When you are finished, submit the document to your instructor as requested.

FIGURE 5-9: Tips for public speaking from experts

"Best way to conquer stage fright is to know what you're talking about."
— Michael H. Mescon

"If you have an important point to make, don't try to be subtle or clever. Use a pile driver. Hit the point once. Then come back and hit it again. Then hit it a third time—a tremendous whack."
— Winston Churchill

"Nothing gives one person so much advantage over another as to remain always cool and unruffled under all circumstances."
— Thomas Jefferson

"Always be shorter than anybody dared to hope."
— Lord Reading

"The most precious things in speech are the pauses."
— Sir Ralph Richardson

"If you can't write your message in a sentence, you can't say it in an hour."
— Dianna Booher

"All the great speakers were bad speakers at first."
— Ralph Waldo Emerson

FIGURE 5-10: Loosen up before you speak

Anne Bæk Pedersen/Photos.com

TABLE 5-5: Managing anxiety do's and don'ts

guidelines	do	don't
Preparation	• Make sure you are well prepared • Loosen up physically before speaking	• **Don't** think you can be effective by improvising instead of preparing • **Don't** continue chewing gum, yawning, or stretching in front of the audience
Speaking	• Breathe fully and relax • Sip water during pauses • Focus on the presentation and the visuals • Act confidently • Remember that the audience wants you to succeed	• **Don't** forget to breathe • **Don't** drink too much water • **Don't** drink milk, caffeinated beverages, or alcohol • **Don't** apologize for small errors • **Don't** talk yourself into feeling apprehensive

Using Appropriate Visuals

As you develop your speech, prepare visual aids that reinforce your major ideas, stimulate your audience, and work well in the physical setting of your presentation. Psychologists and educators have found that people learn more readily and retain more information when learning is reinforced by visualization. Popular visual aids include flip charts, overhead transparencies, slides, and video clips. If visual aids are poorly done, they distract from what you are saying. Well-designed visuals can significantly enhance your presentation. Table 5-6 lists the do's and don'ts for using visuals. Figure 5-11 shows examples of effective visuals. ▸case▸ During your presentation on customer relations, you provide a number of visual aids to clarify your points, improve your audience's comprehension, and keep the information engaging.

1. Include one message per visual

Keep your visuals simple by limiting each to a single message. The dominant idea of each visual should be obvious to the audience immediately. If it takes someone more than five seconds to understand what a visual is communicating, it is too complex. Pictures, graphs, and images should make up most of your visual content.

2. Let your audience read or listen (not both)

Visual aids should not provide reading material while you talk. Use them to illustrate or highlight the points that you are talking about. Avoid the phenomenon known as "Death by PowerPoint," where you display slide after slide of bullet points to your audience. Visuals should not be used as a script or a substitute for a well-rehearsed delivery.

3. Keep the effects simple

Presentation graphics programs such as Microsoft PowerPoint and Apple Keynote include a variety of visual effects that you can use with the slides. The most common effects add visual interest to transitions (the animation between different slides) and builds (the animation used to display elements on a particular slide). Most of these are too involved and should be avoided. If you need to include effects, stick with quick fades and basic dissolves.

QUICK TIP

Use a dark background with light text and graphics, or a light background with dark text and graphics to improve readability.

4. Manage your colors

Color is effective for capturing attention and emphasizing important ideas, but you can overdo it. Don't use more than three colors on a visual. Try to use the same three throughout your presentation for consistency. Use colors to contrast, differentiate categories, separate data, or highlight a key point. Clearly contrast your background and foreground colors.

QUICK TIP

If you want to use a graphic or pattern, choose one that has little difference between its light and dark shades.

5. Use minimalist backgrounds

Don't let the background of your visuals become the foreground. Complex graphics or patterns often have areas where the background color shifts between light and dark. These create a background without a uniform shade and makes contrasting text very difficult to read.

6. Proofread carefully

Displaying a visual with an obviously misspelled word can sink your presentation. An error makes people think you are an amateur and distracts the audience. People will focus on your mistake and stop listening to what you have to say. Proofread every visual carefully and have a trusted friend provide a second opinion.

Practice using appropriate visuals by evaluating the visuals provided for a presentation. Open the VC5-Y38.docx document and follow the steps in the worksheet. When you are finished, submit the document to your instructor as requested.

FIGURE 5-11: Examples of effective visuals

Electronic presentations

Handouts

Flip charts or whiteboards

Video

TABLE 5-6: Using visuals do's and don'ts

guidelines	do	don't
Content	• Use one idea per visual • Make sure your audience can interpret a visual in five seconds • Highlight or illustrate your points	• **Don't** pack too much information into a graphic • **Don't** make your audience spend more than five seconds interpreting a visual • **Don't** include new ideas in a graphic
Effects and formatting	• Use simple transitions and other special effects • Use color to highlight information • Clearly contrast your background and foreground colors	• **Don't** distract your audience from the content with transitions and other visual effects • **Don't** use more than three colors in a single graphic (except for photographs) • **Don't** clutter the background of a graphic with patterns or objects

Managing Questions and Answers

Your business presentation does not end when you finish what you have to say; you are expected to respond to questions from the audience. You can request questions from the audience during your presentation or in a period at the end of your presentation during a question-and-answer session. Handling these questions with authority is part of making a successful presentation, one you should prepare for and rehearse as you do other parts of the session. Figure 5-12 outlines steps to prepare for questions. Table 5-7 lists the do's and don'ts for handling questions and answers. `case` After summarizing the main points of your presentation on customer service at Quest Specialty Travel, you encourage members of the audience to ask questions.

ESSENTIAL ELEMENTS

1. Establish the ground rules

Explain at which points during the presentation you will take questions and how participants will be recognized to speak. Make this clear at the beginning of your presentation if you want people to wait until you've concluded your remarks. Smaller groups expect you to take questions anytime during your speech.

> **QUICK TIP**
> You can also ask your audience a question if they don't have any for you.

2. Kick start the questions

It is awkward to invite questions and not have any asked. You can help start the process by asking your own questions. Start with a statement such as, "A question I am often asked is...." Follow this with your own question and answer.

> **QUICK TIP**
> If you can't hear the question, or some part of it is unclear, ask them to repeat their comment.

3. Listen to the entire question

Wait for the audience member to finish asking the question before you begin your answer. The only exception is when it becomes necessary to interrupt a rambling question or lengthy statement. Instead of letting one person assume control of the session, break in tactfully to keep the entire audience involved. Acknowledge the question or statement and move to the next questioner.

4. Repeat each question

Look the questioner in the eye while they are speaking. Restate the question to make certain that you've understood it correctly. Repeating the question helps those in the audience who may not have heard it initially and gives you extra time to think about your response.

5. Answer to the entire audience

After you've restated the question, break eye contact with the questioner and turn towards the audience. Give your answer to the entire group. Avoid creating a two-person conversation that others in the audience will not feel a part of. Figure 5-13 provides examples of effective ways to respond to questions.

> **QUICK TIP**
> Try opening the question up to the entire audience. Someone will usually have an answer.

6. Don't answer if you don't know

Sometimes you don't know the answer to a particular question. In such cases, avoid trying to bluff or invent a response. Doing so will cost you credibility. Instead, acknowledge that it is a good question, indicate that you'll look into it, and then follow up directly with the questioner.

YOU TRY IT

Practice managing questions and answers by evaluating a question-and-answer session. Open the VC5-Y39.docx document and follow the steps in the worksheet. When you are finished, submit the document to your instructor as requested.

FIGURE 5-12: Preparation steps

Before the presentation
- Anticipate questions
- Rehearse your answers
- Identify questions you most want to hear

During the Q & A period
- Restate the question
- State your position
- Support your position
- Summarize your response
- Make sure the questioner is satisfied

FIGURE 5-13: Answering questions

Defensive response | Open response

"You missed my point." | "Perhaps I wasn't clear. I'll briefly restate that main idea."

"You don't understand the material." | "Let me clarify that point."

"No, that won't work." | "Here's my approach..."

"Is that a serious question?" | "Thanks for asking that."

TABLE 5-7: Managing questions do's and don'ts

guidelines	do	don't
Rules	• At the beginning of your presentation, announce when you will take questions • Indicate how you will recognize audience members to speak	• **Don't** allow the question-and-answer period to drag on; set a time limit • **Don't** postpone questions in a small group
Questions	• Encourage questions by asking and answering one yourself • Listen to the entire question • Provide a microphone or ask the questioner to stand to be heard • Repeat the question so everyone can hear it	• **Don't** invite questions and then quickly end the session if no one poses a question • **Don't** let one person take control of the question period • **Don't** interrupt or talk over the question
Answers	• As you repeat the question, make eye contact with the person who asked it • Answer to the entire audience • Reinforce the main ideas of your presentation • Feel free to admit you don't know the answer to a question and open it to the audience	• **Don't** answer defensively • **Don't** debate with the questioner • **Don't** answer the questioner only • **Don't** attempt to answer if you don't know the correct response

Technology @ Work: Presentation Software

You use presentation software to create and deliver electronic slide shows. Presentation software, Microsoft PowerPoint in particular, has become the standard way to make and give business presentations. Released by Microsoft in 1990, PowerPoint is easily the most well-established of the presentation software tools. In fact, Microsoft estimates that more than 30 million PowerPoint presentations are given each day. You can also use other presentation software, some of which is designed for special circumstances. **case** Nancy McDonald asks you to review the top five programs designed for business presentations.

1. **Microsoft Office PowerPoint**

   Part of the Microsoft Office suite of programs, PowerPoint (*office.microsoft.com/powerpoint*) is widely used in business and education. See Figure 5-14. Detractors say that it dictates the way you communicate by reducing ideas to short bullet points. However, the real culprits are ineffective communicators, not the software tool itself.

2. **Adobe Flash**

   If you want to use sophisticated animation effects and import video, Adobe Flash is an excellent choice (*www.adobe.com/products/flash*). However, Adobe Flash requires training and expertise to produce the effects you want. One advantage of using Adobe Flash is that you can easily publish a presentation online.

3. **Google Docs**

   One of the applications available from Google Docs (*www.google.com/docs*) is called Presentations, a basic tool for creating slide shows. The strength of Presentations is not its features, which are more limited than PowerPoint's. Like other Google applications, Presentations is designed for online collaboration and sharing.

4. **Apple Keynote**

   If you use a Macintosh computer, the tool of choice for presentations is Apple Keynote (*www.apple.com/iwork/keynote*). One impressive feature is called Keynote Remote, which you add to an iPhone or iPod Touch so you can use it as a wireless controller. You can then move around a room in which are presenting, using your iPhone or iPod Touch to control slides and read your slide notes. Figure 5-15 shows Apple Keynote for iOS, which runs on mobile devices.

5. **OpenOffice Impress**

   A free open source presentation tool, OpenOffice Impress (*www.openoffice.org/product/impress.html*) contains some features for editing graphics not available in PowerPoint. For example, Impress provides tools for precisely positioning graphics, adjusting color resolution, and creating and applying styles to graphics. It is also distributed under an open source license, which means it available for download without charge.

Practice working with presentation software. Open the VC5-TechWork.docx document and follow the steps in the worksheet. When you are finished, submit the document to your instructor as requested.

FIGURE 5-14: Microsoft PowerPoint 2010

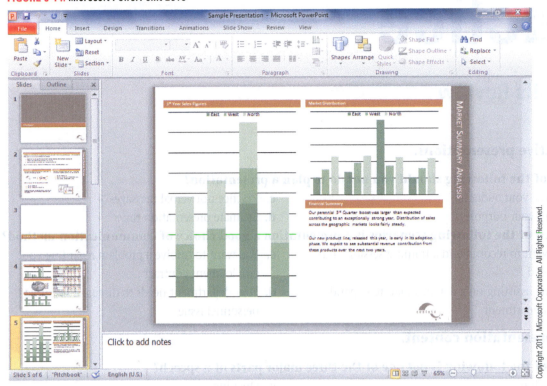

FIGURE 5-15: Apple Keynote for mobile devices

Practice

Soft Skills Review

Plan effective presentations.

1. **Which of the following should you *not* do to plan a presentation?**
   - **a.** Analyze your audience
   - **b.** Clarify your purpose
   - **c.** Practice nonverbal messages
   - **d.** Estimate presentation time

2. **In which of the following scenarios is a presentation a good choice of communication method?**
   - **a.** You want to recommend a training session you attended
   - **b.** You are assisting on a detailed plan to expand your department
   - **c.** You want to resolve a problem regarding your employment contract
   - **d.** Your department needs to discuss a sensitive personnel issue

Develop presentation content.

1. **Which of the following is *not* one of the three major parts of a speech?**
   - **a.** Salutation
   - **b.** Conclusion
   - **c.** Opening
   - **d.** Body

2. **What is a storyboard?**
   - **a.** A board you use to tell stories
   - **b.** An online collection of anecdotes
   - **c.** A template for creating PowerPoint presentations
   - **d.** A planning tool for visualizing presentations

Rehearse your presentation.

1. **A good way to rehearse your presentation is to:**
   - **a.** take frequent sips of water
   - **b.** record yourself on video
   - **c.** develop visual aids
   - **d.** relax and feel free to improvise

2. **What is visualization?**
   - **a.** Stretching exercise
   - **b.** Method of digital video recording
   - **c.** Technique of forming a mental image of yourself performing a task
   - **d.** Technique for rehearsing gestures

Deliver your presentation.

1. **When is it a good idea to use a short pause during your presentation?**
   - **a.** To add emphasis to a key idea
   - **b.** To separate thoughts
   - **c.** To let your audience absorb your words
   - **d.** All of the above

2. **During your presentation, you should:**
   - **a.** use gestures to reinforce what you are saying
   - **b.** remain behind a lectern
   - **c.** move around the room
   - **d.** all of the above

Build rapport.

1. Why should you build rapport with your audience?

    a. So they ask challenging questions

    b. So they are cooperative and interested

    c. So they don't interrupt you

    d. So they can understand your message

2. When you are showing a slide show or video in a darkened room, what should you be sure to do?

    a. Talk to the audience dramatically from a dark part of the room

    b. Read the bullet points on the screen

    c. Illuminate your face

    d. All of the above

Manage anxiety.

1. What does it mean if you suffer performance anxiety before a presentation?

    a. You fear making a mistake in front of others

    b. You did not prepare adequately

    c. You are overprepared

    d. You have an uncommon disorder

2. What can you do during a speech to minimize performance anxiety?

    a. Breathe deeply

    b. Apologize often

    c. Drink caffeinated cola

    d. All of the above

Use appropriate visuals.

1. A single visual should communicate:

    a. a thousand messages

    b. six bullets

    c. a single message

    d. something positive and something negative

2. When designing slides to show during a presentation, you should:

    a. use many lively colors

    b. display a pattern or animation in the background

    c. use simple transitions

    d. use at least two special effects per slide

Manage questions and answers.

1. What ground rules should you establish for asking questions?

    a. You take questions only if time allows

    b. You take questions after the presentation

    c. Questioners cannot refer to notes

    d. If you have a question, ask someone sitting nearby

2. When answering questions, you should:

    a. debate with the questioner

    b. attempt to answer even if you don't know the correct response

    c. direct your response to the questioner

    d. direct your response to the audience

Technology @ work: Presentation software.

1. Which of the following is *not* an example of presentation software?

    a. Microsoft Office PowerPoint

    b. Adobe Flash

    c. Apple Keynote

    d. Adobe Slideshow

2. Which of the following is an advantage of using OpenOffice Impress?

    a. It is distributed under an open source license

    b. It is designed for online presentation

    c. It is the popular with Macintosh users

    d. It is designed for collaboration and sharing

Critical Thinking Questions

1. You are attending your manager's presentation and notice that she is not following many of the basic guidelines for creating and delivering presentations. In particular, she is reading her slide notes verbatim and doesn't have many visuals, just bullet points. What should you do?

2. Edward Tufte is a statistician and professor at Yale University. The *New York Times* describes him as "the da Vinci of Data." He argues that PowerPoint "actively facilitates the making of lightweight presentations." Do you agree or disagree?

3. Suppose you have always had terrible stage fright. You are among the finalists interviewing for a job and learn that giving occasional oral presentations is part of the job description. Should you take the job if offered? Why or why not?

4. One of the quotations included in this unit is by Ralph Waldo Emerson, a 19th-century American essayist, philosopher, and poet, who said, "All the great speakers were bad speakers at first." How do you think those speakers developed from bad to great?

5. You are giving a presentation advocating that your company sponsor the local qualifying events for the next summer Olympics, a position you strongly support. A member of your audience is becoming openly hostile to your presentation and is challenging your points. What do you do?

Independent Challenge 1

You work in the Customer Service Department at NorthStar, a four-season resort in eastern Maine. The owners of the resort are building condominiums near the golf course and are ready to attract potential buyers. Kelly Mortensen, a supervisor at the resort, asks you to help her plan a presentation promoting the condominiums. She has prepared the outline shown in Figure 5-16.

a. Open the **VC5-IC1.docx** document and follow the steps in the worksheet.

b. Proofread the document carefully to fix any grammar or formatting errors.

c. Submit the document to your instructor as requested.

FIGURE 5-16

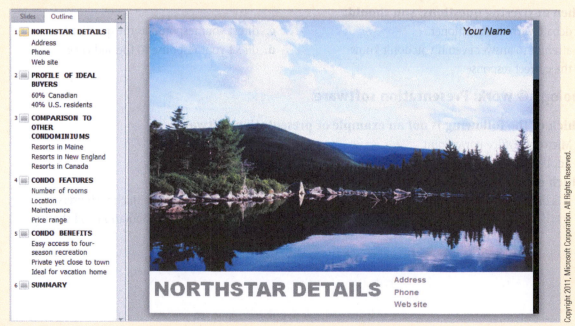

Independent Challenge 2

You work in the Bloomington Health Clinic, a family practice clinic in Bloomington, Indiana. As a patient service representative, you talk to patients and help solve their problems. You are developing a presentation on first aid that you will give to local high school students. Figure 5-17 shows the current presentation and its outline.

a. Open the **VC5-IC2.docx** document and follow the steps in the worksheet.

b. Proofread the document carefully to fix any grammar or formatting errors.

c. Submit the document to your instructor as requested.

FIGURE 5-17

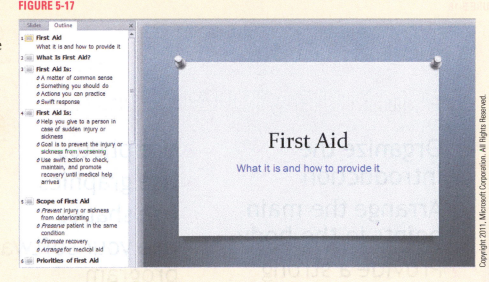

Real Life Independent Challenge

This Real Life Independent Challenge requires an Internet connection.

You are preparing for a job search and are researching job opportunities on the Web. You want to share your findings with other students. Using any presentation tool described in the Technology @ Work: Presentation Software lesson, create a presentation that answers the following questions (not necessarily in this order). Save the presentation, proofread it carefully, and then submit it to your instructor as requested.

a. What tools do online job sites provide for current students and recent graduates?

b. What are the pros and cons of three job sites you visited?

c. What are three fields where job opportunities are high?

d. What types of skills are employers looking for in these fields?

Team Challenge

You work for the Global Village, an import/export company specializing in products made from sustainable materials. Your company is committed to preserving natural resources around the world, especially in developing countries. Your supervisor asks you and the others in your department to create a 10-minute presentation on sustainable building and architecture. As a team, meet to discuss the following topics:

- What is sustainable building? How can you find out more about this topic?
- What are the most important issues in sustainable building and architecture?
- How will each team member contribute to the presentation?
- What visual aids will you use during the presentation?
- What software tool will you use to develop and deliver the presentation?

a. After discussing these topics and assigning roles, work independently on your part of the presentation.

b. Meet at least once as a group to review and rehearse the presentation.

c. Save the presentation, proofread it carefully, and then submit it to your instructor as requested.

Be the Critic

Review the slide shown in Figure 5-18, which provides pointers on giving presentations. Analyze the slide, noting its weaknesses, and send a list of the weaknesses to your instructor.

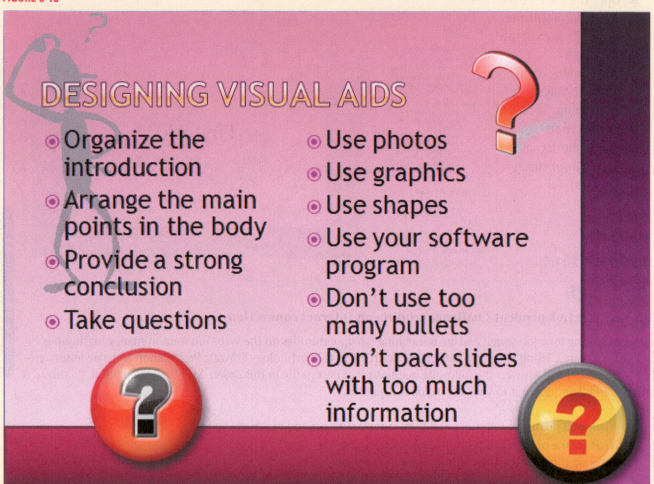

Glossary

Active listening Concentrating on a speaker's words without allowing yourself to be distracted.

Caller ID A telephone system feature that displays the phone number and sometimes the name of the caller.

Channel The medium used to communicate with others, such as voice, telephone, e-mail, or letters.

Closed question A specific, concrete question that generally seeks a "yes" or "no" answer and is asked when a direct answer is needed.

Customer service The practices used in an organization's relationship with its customers: meeting their expectations, listening to their statements, and solving their problems.

Decode To interpret a message and understand it.

Digital video recorder A camera that records video in a format you can play on your computer.

Empathy The capacity to understand another person's feelings or state of mind.

Ethics Principles for acceptable conduct; honest, fair behavior and decisions. Ethics also involves the moral obligations you have to treat others as you want to be treated.

Feedback question A question asked about the conversation or problem-solving process itself to determine what is important to someone.

Follow-up question A question asked in response to an answer that someone else provides. Follow-up questions are intended to discover more information or elicit an opinion.

Glossophobia The fear of public speaking, which is the most common of all human phobias.

Internet monitoring tool Software that monitors the Internet for activities and comments related to a specific topic, usually a product or service.

IP phone A telephone device that lets you connect directly to a network without using a computer.

Meeting An activity that involves three or more people gathering to exchange information, make decisions, and solve problems.

Microblog An online service that lets you exchange very short messages with others by combining the features of blogging, text messaging, and social networking.

Mirroring Mimicking the body language and gestures of a person you are trying to persuade.

Negotiation A form of communication through which two or more people with different needs and goals try to identify a mutually acceptable solution to a problem.

Office politics The interactions and relationships between people within an organization, usually focused on who is gaining or losing power and influence.

Open-ended question A question without a particular answer usually asked to encourage another person to articulate motivations, ideas, and solutions.

Performance anxiety The discomfort felt in anticipation of performing or speaking in front of an audience.

Persuasion Communication that guides other people towards the adoption of an idea or action.

Pitch A sound or speech quality that varies in the frequency of vibration.

Proximity In communication, how physically close you are to your audience.

Rapport Mutual trust, emotional similarity, and natural personal attraction.

Rhetorical triangle A diagram that shows how your speaking ability depends on how well you appeal to your audience in terms of logics, ethics, and emotions.

Screening When answering the phone, restricting transfers to certain callers and taking messages from others to avoid interrupting busy people.

Softphone Software that you install on a computer so you can make VoIP calls without a special telephone device.

Stage fright *See* Performance anxiety.

Tact The ability to act or speak in a way that maintains good relations with others or avoids giving offense.

Telephony The technology for electronically transmitting voice across distances.

Tweet A text message of up to 140 characters.

Verbal communication Communication in which one person sends a message to another person or group using speech and the speaker and listener understand each other. Also called oral communication.

Visualization The technique of forming a mental image or vision of yourself performing a task.

Vocal element A characteristic of the way you speak, such as voice inflection, rate of speech, volume, or tone.

Voice over Internet Protocol (VoIP) A telephone technology that allows you to make phone calls using your high-speed Internet connection so that your voice travels across the Internet as data, similar to e-mail.

Voice-mail system A system that connects telephones to computers that store messages, play a prerecorded announcement to callers, and allow them to record a short message.

Web conferencing Using an Internet-connected computer to meet with others and communicate orally. Group members can share ideas and view the same material on a computer screen or whiteboard without physically traveling to the same location.

Index

A

accounts, Twitter, Verbal Communication 90
accuracy of messages, Verbal Communication 8, Verbal Communication 9, Verbal Communication 14, Verbal Communication 58
active listening, Verbal Communication 76–77
Adobe Flash, Verbal Communication 114
agendas
  meeting, Verbal Communication 84–85
  for phone calls, Verbal Communication 50
alerts, Google, Verbal Communication 40–41
Americans with Disabilities Amendments Act, Verbal Communication 39
Anderson, Douglas, Verbal Communication 5
anger
  handling angry customers, Verbal Communication 34–35
  managing conflict, Verbal Communication 82–83
apologies to customers, Verbal Communication 34
Apple Keynote, Verbal Communication 110, Verbal Communication 114–115
Aristotle, Verbal Communication 8
Aristotle's triangle (fig.), Verbal Communication 9
articulation, Verbal Communication 4, Verbal Communication 5
audience
  analyzing for presentations, Verbal Communication 98–99
  proximity to, Verbal Communication 6
  question-and-answer sessions, Verbal Communication 112–113
  types, Verbal Communication 105

B

balancing viewpoints, Verbal Communication 14, Verbal Communication 15
body language
  See also nonverbal language
  of success, Verbal Communication 7
Booher, Dianna, Verbal Communication 109

C

caller ID, Verbal Communication 48
cell phones
  See also telephone communication
  do's and don'ts (table), Verbal Communication 63
  etiquette, Verbal Communication 62–63
channels, **Verbal Communication 4**
Churchill, Winston, Verbal Communication 109
clarity
  credibility do's and don'ts (table), Verbal Communication 9
  of messages, Verbal Communication 12–13
  striving for, Verbal Communication 8
  understanding customer problems, Verbal Communication 30
clichés, avoiding, Verbal Communication 16

clients, introducing, Verbal Communication 88–89
closed questions, **Verbal Communication 30**, Verbal Communication 31
communications
  cross-cultural issues, Verbal Communication 16–17
  empathic, Verbal Communication 28–29
  ethics and, Verbal Communication 14–15
  informal. See informal communication
  telephone. See telephone communication
  verbal. See verbal communications
conflict management, Verbal Communication 82–83
consistency of messages, Verbal Communication 14
credibility
  developing, Verbal Communication 8
  do's and don'ts (table), Verbal Communication 9
  establishing, Verbal Communication 79
cross-cultural communication issues, Verbal Communication 16–17
crucial conversations, Verbal Communication 3
customer service, **Verbal Communication 26**
  basics, do's and don'ts (table), Verbal Communication 26–27
  dealing with unexpected, Verbal Communication 36–37
  denying requests, Verbal Communication 32–33
  disabled customers, working with, Verbal Communication 38–39
  handling angry customers, Verbal Communication 34–35
  Internet monitoring, Verbal Communication 40–41
  representatives, Verbal Communication 33
  working with the disabled, Verbal Communication 38–39
customers
  disabled, working with, Verbal Communication 38–39
  handling angry, Verbal Communication 34–35
  introducing, Verbal Communication 88–89
  keeping informed about problems, Verbal Communication 36
  working with, Verbal Communication 25

D

decode, **Verbal Communication 2**
delivering presentations, Verbal Communication 104–105
denying customer requests, Verbal Communication 32–33
digital video recorder, **Verbal Communication 102**

E

Ecker, Juanita, Verbal Communication 75
e-mail
  vs. telephone communication, Verbal Communication 49
  when to use, Verbal Communication 12
emergencies, handling, Verbal Communication 36–37
Emerson, Ralph Waldo, Verbal Communication 109

empathy
  communicating empathetically, Verbal Communication 28–39
  described, Verbal Communication 8, **Verbal Communication 28**
enthusiasm, Verbal Communication 36, Verbal Communication 37
ethics, and communicating, Verbal Communication 14–15
etiquette
  cell phone, Verbal Communication 62–63
  meeting, Verbal Communication 84–85
  telephone, Verbal Communication 39
  text message, Verbal Communication 53
  voice mail, Verbal Communication 13
eye contact, Verbal Communication 3, Verbal Communication 6, Verbal
  Communication 106

F

facts vs. opinions, Verbal Communication 14, Verbal Communication 15
feedback, Verbal Communication 9
  and active listening, Verbal Communication 76
  do's and don'ts (table), Verbal Communication 11
  examples of positive, negative (fig.), Verbal Communication 11
  giving and receiving, Verbal Communication 10–11
  from spoken communications, Verbal Communication 3
  telephone conversations, Verbal Communication 48
feedback questions, **Verbal Communication 30**, Verbal Communication 31
following others on Twitter, Verbal Communication 90
follow-up questions, **Verbal Communication 30**, Verbal Communication 31

G

Gallo, Carmine, Verbal Communication 7, Verbal Communication 105
gestures
  appropriate, Verbal Communication 6
  in presentations, Verbal Communication 104–105
glossophobia, **Verbal Communication 108**
goals, and effective negotiations, Verbal Communication 80–81
Google Alerts, monitoring Internet usage with, Verbal
  Communication 40–41
Google Docs, Verbal Communication 114
Gore, Al, Verbal Communication 105
GoToMeeting Web conferencing software, Verbal Communication 18–19
greetings, Verbal Communication 3, Verbal Communication 54–55

H

handicapped, working with the, Verbal Communication 38–39
health, safety, Verbal Communication 36
holding phone calls, Verbal Communication 60–61

I

idioms, avoiding, Verbal Communication 16
informal communication
  introductions, Verbal Communication 88–89
  managing conflict, Verbal Communication 82–83
  meeting participation, Verbal Communication 84–85
  microblogging tools, Verbal Communication 90–91
  negotiating effectively, Verbal Communication 80–81
  obstacles to (table), Verbal Communication 75

  office politics, Verbal Communication 86–87
  overview of, Verbal Communication 73–75
  speaking persuasively, Verbal Communication 78–79
Internet monitoring tools, **Verbal Communication 40**
interruptions, reducing, Verbal Communication 57, Verbal
  Communication 62–63
introductions
  making proper, Verbal Communication 88–89
  on phone calls, Verbal Communication 50, Verbal Communication 51,
    Verbal Communication 52
invitations to Web conferences, Verbal Communication 18
IP phones, **Verbal Communication 64**

J

Jefferson, Thomas, Verbal Communication 109

K

Keynote Remote, Verbal Communication 114

L

language
  listener-centered, Verbal Communication 28
  understanding nonverbal, Verbal Communication 6–7
  using inoffensive, Verbal Communication 38
  vague vs. clear (fig.), Verbal Communication 13
listening, **Verbal Communication 26**
  actively, Verbal Communication 76–77
  customer service do's and don'ts (table), Verbal Communication 27
  using listener-centered language, Verbal Communication 28

M

meetings, **Verbal Communication 84**
  introductions, Verbal Communication 88–89
  office politics, Verbal Communication 86–87
  participating in, Verbal Communication 84–85
Mescon, Michael H., Verbal Communication 109
messages
  clarity, Verbal Communication 12–13
  consistency, Verbal Communication 14
  contributing at meetings, Verbal Communication 84
  customer service do's and don'ts (table), Verbal Communication 27
  depersonalizing negative, Verbal Communication 10
  leaving professional, Verbal Communication 56–57
  making clear, Verbal Communication 12–13
  organizing, Verbal Communication 2–3
  outgoing, Verbal Communication 55
  posting tweets, Verbal Communication 90
  simplicity, Verbal Communication 2, Verbal Communication 16
  taking other people's calls, Verbal Communication 58–59
  text. *See* text messages
microblogging tools, Verbal Communication 90–91
microblogs described, **Verbal Communication 90**
Microsoft Live Meeting, Verbal Communication 18
Microsoft PowerPoint, Verbal Communication 110, Verbal
  Communication 114–115

mirroring, and persuasive speaking, **Verbal Communication 78**
monitoring Internet usage, **Verbal Communication 40**

negative feedback, Verbal Communication 11
negative messages, depersonalizing, Verbal Communication 10
negotiation
  described, **Verbal Communication 80**
  negotiating effectively, Verbal Communication 80–81
nonverbal language
  and active listening, Verbal Communication 76–77
  do's and don'ts (table), Verbal Communication 7, Verbal
    Communication 13
  understanding, Verbal Communication 6–7
  when responding to customer request, Verbal Communication 32

office politics
  dealing with, do's and don'ts, Verbal Communication 86–87
  described, **Verbal Communication 86**
Office PowerPoint, Verbal Communication 114–115
open-ended questions, **Verbal Communication 30**, Verbal
    Communication 31
OpenOffice Impress presentation software, Verbal Communication 114
opinion vs. fact, Verbal Communication 14, Verbal Communication 15
organizations
  office politics, and company culture, Verbal Communication 86–87
  purpose of informal communication in, Verbal Communication 74–75
organizing messages, Verbal Communication 2–3
outgoing messages, Verbal Communication 55

performance anxiety, **Verbal Communication 108**
persuasion
  described, **Verbal Communication 78**
  techniques do's and don'ts (table), Verbal Communication 79
phone calls
  See also telephone communication
  placing, Verbal Communication 50–51
  receiving, Verbal Communication 52–53
  screening, holding, transferring, Verbal Communication 60–61
  taking calls do's and don'ts (table), Verbal Communication 59
  taking for other people, Verbal Communication 58–59
  telephone etiquette, Verbal Communication 39
  voice mail, Verbal Communication 54–57
  voice mail etiquette, Verbal Communication 13
physical distractions, reducing, Verbal Communication 12, Verbal
    Communication 13
pitch, **Verbal Communication 4**, Verbal Communication 5
positive feedback, Verbal Communication 11
posture, maintaining good, Verbal Communication 6, Verbal
    Communication 7
PowerPoint 2010, Verbal Communication 114–115
preparing for presentations, Verbal Communication 98–99, Verbal
    Communication 108

presentations
  appropriate visuals, Verbal Communication 110–111
  backup plans, Verbal Communication 104
  delivering, Verbal Communication 104–105
  developing content, Verbal Communication 100–101
  making formal, Verbal Communication 97
  managing anxiety, Verbal Communication 108–109
  managing questions and answers, Verbal Communication 112–113
  planning effective, Verbal Communication 98–99
  rapport, building, Verbal Communication 106–107
  rehearsing, Verbal Communication 102–103
  software for, Verbal Communication 114–115
problems
  asking questions to understand, Verbal Communication 30–31
  dealing with unexpected, Verbal Communication 36–37
  managing conflict, Verbal Communication 82–83
professional messages, leaving, Verbal Communication 56–57
proofreading presentations, Verbal Communication 110
proximity, **Verbal Communication 6**
public speaking
  building confidence in, Verbal Communication 5
  managing anxiety, Verbal Communication 108–109
  presentations. *See* presentations
  speaking persuasively, Verbal Communication 78–79

questions
  and active listening, Verbal Communication 76
  and answers in presentations, Verbal Communication 112–113
  asking to understand problems, Verbal Communication 30–31
  in customer service, Verbal Communication 26
  disabled customers, Verbal Communication 38
  do's and don'ts (table), Verbal Communication 31

R

rapport, **Verbal Communication 106**
  building during presentations, Verbal Communication 106–107
  establishing, Verbal Communication 30
Reading, Lord, Verbal Communication 109
recording presentation rehearsals, Verbal Communication 102
rehearsing
  phone calls to customers, Verbal Communication 50
  presentations, Verbal Communication 12, Verbal Communication 102–103
  receiving phone calls, Verbal Communication 52–53
  rehearsal do's and don'ts (table), Verbal Communication 103
relationships, strengthening with informal communication, Verbal
    Communication 74
rephrasing customer requests, Verbal Communication 32–33
requests, denying customer, Verbal Communication 32–33
responsibilities in unexpected situations, Verbal Communication 36–37
returning calls, Verbal Communication 54–55
rhetorical triangle, **Verbal Communication 8**
Richardson, Sir Ralph, Verbal Communication 109
ringtones, annoying, Verbal Communication 62

S

safety, health, Verbal Communication 36
screening phone calls, **Verbal Communication 60**, Verbal
   Communication 61
Skype
   using, Verbal Communication 65
   VoIP provider, Verbal Communication 64
slides in presentations, Verbal Communication 99
softphones, Verbal Communication 64
software, presentation, Verbal Communication 114
spoken communications
   See also verbal communications
   appropriate uses for (table), Verbal Communication 3
   pauses, effective, Verbal Communication 105
   three parts of speeches, Verbal Communication 100
   vocal elements, using effectively, Verbal Communication 4–5
stage fright, Verbal Communication 108
storyboards
   described, **Verbal Communication 100**
   developing presentation content, Verbal Communication 100–101

T

tact, Verbal Communication 10
telephone communication
   vs. e-mail, Verbal Communication 49
   leaving professional messages, Verbal Communication 56–57
   overview of, Verbal Communication 48–49
   phone calls do's and don'ts (table), Verbal Communication 51, Verbal
      Communication 53, Verbal Communication 55
   placing calls, Verbal Communication 50–51
   receiving calls, Verbal Communication 52–53
   reducing interruptions, Verbal Communication 57
   taking other people's calls, Verbal Communication 58–59
   voice-mail systems, Verbal Communication 54–55
telephone etiquette, Verbal Communication 13, Verbal Communication 39
telephony, Verbal Communication 48
10 Simple Secrets of the World's Greatest Business Communicators (Gallo),
   Verbal Communication 7

text messages, Verbal Communication 53
transferring phone calls, Verbal Communication 60–61
Twain, Mark, Verbal Communication 98
tweets, Verbal Communication 90
Twitter, Verbal Communication 90

U

unexpected, dealing with, Verbal Communication 36–37

V

verbal communications, **Verbal Communication 2**
   See also spoken communications, Verbal Communication 30
   basics of, Verbal Communication 1
   cross-cultural issues, Verbal Communication 16–17
   pace and pauses (table), Verbal Communication 5
   rapport, establishing, Verbal Communication 30
   voice pitch, Verbal Communication 4
video-taping presentation rehearsals, Verbal Communication 102–103
visualization, Verbal Communication 102
visuals
   planning, Verbal Communication 18
   using in presentations, Verbal Communication 100–101, Verbal
      Communication 110–111
vocal elements, Verbal Communication 4, Verbal Communication 5
voice mail, Verbal Communication 13
Voice over Internet Protocol (VoIP), Verbal Communication 64, Verbal
   Communication 65
voice-mail systems, Verbal Communication 54

W

Web conferencing
   described, **Verbal Communication 18**
   examples of (figs.), Verbal Communication 19
WebEx Web conferencing software, Verbal Communication 18–19